INCANDESCENCE
Rising Above Darkness

Memoir & Art
by
Author Artist
Clare Cooley

INCANDESCENSE
Rising Above Darkness
By Clare Cooley
FIRST PAPERBACK EDITION (Full Color)

ISBN 978-1-7370762-0-9
Copyright © MotherSon Productions LLC 2021

MotherSon Productions

Book designed by Clare Cooley and Bodhi Werner
All art including the cover by Clare Cooley
For photo credits see Special Thanks

Please join the mailing list for more information about *Incandescence*
www.IncandescenceBook.com

Follow *Incandescence* on Social Media
Facebook
Facebook.com/IncandescenceBook

Instagram
Instagram.com/Incandescence_Book

To view or purchase Clare Cooley's Art
www.ClareCooley.com/shop

To see a short documentary about Clare's work "Life of Art"
www.MotherSonProductions.com

For more information about working with Clare,
as a creativity coach, speaking engagements,
art or design commissions, and any other inquiries
ClareCooleyCollection@Gmail.com

Dedication

To my mother, who always called me dear,
which I never tire of repeating.
She is my north star—
I'm grateful for her loving compassion
that set my course to live a life
of kindness, honesty, and being awake.

I feel my mother's pride rising from the water
where we sprinkled her ashes.
Her legacy of love flows around us in rivers, seas,
and in the rain washing away confusion.
Her compassion is the constant
in an ever-changing sea of uncertainty.
In her still water I see my reflection
offering others what she gave me.

Lady In The Dunes

Epigraph

"A life guided through the dark by the light from within is never lost."
Bodhi Werner—Movie Maker

How The Book's Title Came To Be

A friend suggested the title for this book
from a note my mother sent me asking,
"Did you know you have inner incandescence, dear?"

Table of Contents

Introduction

"You saved my life." Mike's words stunned me with the realization that sharing my own story of rising above challenges had helped him rise above his own. Not sure what to say, I gave him a long hug. As the tourists crowded around to take pictures of us dance skaters, I recalled the many times I had heard similar things. I am aware now that telling my story is a way to heal myself and help others. Many have suggested I write my stories to share with others because hearing them helped them stay hopeful. This literary journey set my course on facing my enormous fear of exposing my deep vulnerabilities.

A judge dating my friend once asked, "Her story could have been from a woman on death row. How did she end up so nice?" Perhaps it is because I believe we are not what happens to us, but what we do with it.

Once, an eight-year-old girl was secretly listening in as I read one of my personal experiences to a friend. That evening, the girl asked her mother to invite me to dinner. The girl took me on a tour of their house and, after some time, shared the story of her own assault. I was the first person she had ever told. She felt ashamed of what had happened to her and was confused because her abuser had been a friend.

I told her, "It is confusing, but if we admit it happened, it need not have power over us, and what we get through makes us stronger."

With bright confidence, she said, "I knew you were the one to tell!" I came to see that all it took for her to share her sad secret was hearing that I went through a similar betrayal of trust. Healing can be that simple and sweet. Whenever we tell our truth, even if just to ourselves, we can gain perspective, strength, and healing—a gift we can give ourselves and others.

A woman who asked to read some stories passed them to her sister. The sister called to tell me her husband was a better person after she came home and found him in the backyard weeping after reading them. I started to understand it would be selfish not to share them and began the arduous work of writing and publishing my stories.

Recalling the adversity I have overcome has been difficult but worth it for my healing. Hopefully, I can assist others on their journeys.

On the way here, I have been without my own home. I have lived in a tent, a tepee, in my tiny Renault. I spent a year in an RV and even once lived alone in an abandoned building. I started my first job at fourteen, delivering newspapers on my bicycle. After that, I flipped burgers and served milkshakes as a carhop. I was a receptionist. I sewed in a factory, cleaned houses, made custom clothing, and planted trees. I made sheepskin coats, loaded ships, and then became a janitor. I waitressed, framed pictures, and managed a restaurant. I now sell my art, teach, and have become a creativity coach.

My childhood was heavily influenced by my father's brutality fueled by alcoholism, and my mother's saintly generous spirit hampered by her severe illness. The dynamics of my dysfunctional family resulted in no one noticing I stopped attending school regularly at seven years old. I survived a sexual assault that made me a mother at sixteen. As an adult, I endured a fourteen-year-long divorce from my ex-husband, an attorney, who had total control over all our assets.

This book endeavors to share how I waded through the most difficult of times and triumphed to thrive in a lovely home, filled with my serene art and decor, working joyously with my movie-making son, Bodhi.

I set out to transform my post-traumatic stress into post-traumatic strength and give my pain a higher purpose. It would be a great honor to encourage others to do the same and turn their adversity into their advantage.

My art is inspired by a desire to contemplate natural beauty. My hope is to portray nature's splendor and mystery to help us come back into balance with our precious world. My love of cranes took me from my self taught art to meeting all 15 species of cranes in person and then having my art and writing published by Pomegranite Art Books in the Book Of Cranes.

Being asked to teach my own curriculum, "Dancing into the Arts," to every grade level of the public schools, at universities, drug rehabilitation centers, psychiatric hospitals, crisis shelters, juvenile halls, and with the participants of mental health and drug courts ironically taught me how to be a student. When we listen, feel, express honestly and respectfully, we connect and can learn and teach. I believe continuing to learn is the best way to teach, which is why I think of myself as a guide. While guiding others in multimedia creativity, I experience what I believe to be true—we are all creative. The duality of dark and light is the thread that runs through the fabric of life, which is reflected in all my art forms.

I have learned from working with therapists, probation officers, lawyers, judges, nurses, and many other types of groups and individuals that the fortunate have their imaginations nurtured. A few stay connected to it, and many lose touch with it in this often critical world. As a creativity coach, it is my duty and privilege to guide people home to themselves. There they rediscover joy, the life enhancing resources of imagination and creative expression, and they can heal.

Through my wide variety of jobs, I have observed that everyone wants to be heard and treated respectfully. Across all walks of life, from stressed corporate executives, to patients on their way to electro-shock therapy, I saw the healing power of allowing people to express themselves. When the patient chose not to do shock therapy after our session and continued improving, I became committed to the work. Seeing the profound positive effect of self expression through creativity gave my life the focus to assist or inspire people to enhance their connection to their creativity.

I watched a kindergartner try a new art for the first time and feel pure joy. I saw adults access that same sort of inner happiness. A doctor who began my creativity retreat with doubts and resistance said at the end, "I have not had this much fun since kindergarten!"

One participant realized they needed to quit their unsatisfying job to pursue their artistic passion. Helping people from all backgrounds reconnect with their creativity has shown me the immense value in simply enjoying our own imaginations. It is a deeply satisfying privilege for me to give a gift that can keep on giving.

May the words and chapters that follow help you or someone you care about remain hopeful, survive, and thrive in this beautiful world with all its uncertainties and challenges.

We are not what happens to us, but what we do with it.

Foreword

When I met Clare in her home studio, she exuded warmth, kindness, and light. I experienced immediate trust as she provided a creativity retreat and coaching that was transformative and helped make my vision of writing remembrance poetry a reality. I was honored when she asked me to provide feedback on the book you are about to read.

Incandescence is a collection of fifty-two extraordinary stories of Clare's life that are equally wise and enjoyable. These are stories of possibilities that grew out of challenges, and she shares how she built a life of peace and beauty from chaos. She describes in the story "Duality Dance" how her world had strong light and dark elements: "The contrast between my safe mother and my dangerous father was the ever-present rhythm of my early life the ever-present paradox of my mother being full of selfless purpose and my father being full of selfish pain."

Clare's varied stories include how she learned from the natural world at an early age; survived sexual assault and pregnancy as a teen; found ways to make a living, including work as a longshoreman; and thrived after leaving an abusive long-term relationship. Later chapters describe how she and her adult son journeyed by RV throughout the United States in search of truth and beauty. Her last story, "Nomad Comes Home," describes how they chose Duluth, Minnesota, on Lake Superior as their home.

A theme throughout is Clare's intimate connection with nature and her love of beauty. She writes as if she is painting each page. Her connection to the natural world provided nurturance as she faced near-insurmountable challenges. She tells us how she was able to paint beautiful images of cranes out of her pain.

Clare's writings make the reader feel like she or he received a letter from an intimate friend. I trust you will feel a connection to the author and, in some way, be transformed. Enjoy!

Cathy Cato—BSN, MPH, Poet

Quotes About The Author

"Clare Cooley's true-life story is a riveting and intensely textural journey of amazing adventure, profound creativity, and punishing endurance through unimaginable life events. Cooley is fueled by her amazing spirit, artistic exploration, and an outright will to thrive, not just survive, over a lifetime of extreme challenges. Although her story is harsh and disturbing at times, it is also filled with beauty, inspiration, and life lessons for all."
    Mark Eveslage—Emmy Award-Winning Cinematographer

"I am delighted that Clare Cooley is publishing her book of life stories. Reading her stories, my response is, "WOW!" As a writer, she has her own unique and articulate voice. Her collection of stories is an entertaining and empowering must-read. It is a dramatic story of a person rising above tremendous obstacles using creativity. The subject matter is timely and can help many."
    Claire Kirch—Publishing Industry Veteran

"*Incandescence* is the transformative book for our times, taking us from a dark and hopeless state to an iridescent and wondrous awareness borne by loss and humility, infused by a profound connection to the natural world, and forged by love's indomitable spirit."
    Sumner Matteson—Author of *Afield: Portraits of Wisconsin Naturalists, Empowering Leopold's Legacy*

"If it is possible to turn one's life into a work of art, Clare Cooley has surely done this. Born with extraordinary gifts, Clare has also faced extraordinary odds but met them with truth, beauty and unrelenting courage. May she be an example of grace under pressure and may her memoir inspire you to live your truth and always always always remain true to yourself. The wisdom in Clare's *Incandescence* is a guiding light for us all."
    Brenda Knight—Author of *Random Acts of Kindness*

"Clare Cooley gives her stories to help heal, whether on a personal level or collectively. Her kind, strong, and truthful voice shines through as brightly as her works of art."
Lisa Fitzpatrick—Director of Motion & Media Across Disciplines Lab & VIZ Lab, University of Minnesota-Duluth

"In one of my favorite *Star Trek* episodes, "Darmok and Gillard at Tanagra," Captain Picard is stranded on a planet with an alien that communicates through storytelling. My mother's natural way is like this alien, communicating stories from her unique life relevant to the conversation.

I have seen the effects her stories have on people and heard many say they helped them. Some claim they saved their lives. My mother's stories are engaging, authentic, sometimes difficult, always entertaining, and important. I am inspired to share them through my art, cinema, and adapting them into an episodic series."
Bodhi Werner—Movie Maker

"Some who are assaulted lose gentleness; but not Clare."
Josephine Landor—Artist

"No one can go through what Clare has without being profoundly affected. She transformed it into depth."
Jonathan Rice—Co-Founder K.Q.E.D. Public TV S.F.

"Clare keeps challenging herself, which is why she has so much to share."
Walter Landor—Founder of International Design, Landor & Associates

"Some rely on beauty and are selfish. Clare has stayed beautifully selfless."
Mattalyn Pitts—Designer

Statement About The Art

The art between each story is meant to provide a moment of wordless meditation. Except for a few stories the art has no literal connection to the story. I am including it because spending time in creative reverie is how I not only survived, but learned to thrive. Creative expression helped me transform my adversity into advantage—art.

Nature is the subject of my art because it offers us sanctuary. I hope my art gives a voice to the natural world . inspiring us to live in harmony with it, each other, and all creatures.

Note: The Table of Contents shows the story number, the story title, then the title of the art piece.

1
Duality Dance

The duality dance of my life began with the monsoon rains drumming on the thin tin roof of our Quonset hut in the desert. The constant dance between light and dark, inspiration and struggle, serenity and chaos surrounded me as my individuality came into existence. The contrast between my safe mother and my dangerous father was the ever-present rhythm of my early life, the ever-present paradox of my mother being full of selfless purpose and my father being full of selfish pain.

Her life was one of focused care; his life was one of unfocused rage. Her love tried to protect; his fear tried to control. She was a familiar ally; he was an ominous stranger. My mother was guided by the indefinable; my father could not believe in anything he could not define. She was guided by heart; he was led by mind. One was always serene; the other never rested.

During the rainy season, the desert sky could change violently without warning. The stillness of the steady sun could dissolve suddenly into a torrential downpour. Flash floods following the heavy rain could wash away everything in its path. My father's discontent could wash away my mother's calm. I had to learn to dance with the duality. In order not to be swept away by the paradox, I made it a pal and played with it.

My mother had me, an infant with colic, as well as two other toddlers. Her severe asthma and drunk husband made my constant pain and inability to eat too much to handle. My godparents took me in to give my mother a break. My godmother told me, "Everyone tried to comfort you. Anyone who came to visit would go into the room where you were whimpering, and instead of getting you to stop crying, they would come out of the room weeping. You were so tiny and inconsolable. Everyone was devastated. Then one day, the pain in your belly lifted, and you could eat. From that day on, you were happy and self-sufficient."

Pain puts things in perspective. Hurting can be a blessing because when it lifts, everything is easier. My godmother told me all she had to do was give me something new to explore every so often, and I would be content by myself in my playpen.

Eventually, I returned to my parents, but I never felt at home with my father. I never sat on his lap or went to him with a bad dream, a wound, or a tale of a bully.

I was always at home with my mother. She was my sacred witness from whom I never needed to keep secrets. My father showed off his mind at every opportunity, and asking him for any clarification only led to more confusion. They said he was a genius, but he came up with no solutions for his own misery. His brilliance served only to brilliantly outwit himself. His cleverness caught his happiness in a trap of his own making.

My mother never flaunted her intelligence. She spoke at whatever level the person she was talking to was comfortable with.

My father's rage, like a monsoon, could wash away anything in its path. But somewhere deep within me, I knew a man's softness. Perhaps it was my godfather holding me in those first few months.

My mother managed spiritual equilibrium through forgiving everyone all of the time for everything. This enraged my father, as he could not force her to join him in his bitterness and self-loathing. He hated that she loved no matter what.

I survived by silently observing and by dancing alone to feel some joy. I did not engage unless I sensed someone's safety was at risk. When I felt impending conflict, I would distract my father and redirect his destructive energy. I understood the damage he could do. I did not allow it to frighten or anger or cloud my judgment. From a very young age, I practiced stepping aside and letting the hostility trip itself. It was my own sort of spiritual Aikido.

I understood he endured greater pain than he caused others. I knew he had not invented the pain, but he had inherited it from someone else, who had inherited it from someone else before them. Perhaps it was the first pain ever felt by anyone still being passed down. I saw two possibilities for pain: bear it and expand myself or pass it on and expand the pain.

Perhaps being born with colic showed me what my father never considered: we can find a place outside ourselves to absorb all the suffering. My father's life was a series of unsuccessful attempts to distract himself from his anguish. He searched his whole life to find what my mother had without going anywhere. He climbed mountains, scuba dived, and raced cars, chasing the peace my mother found without doing anything but loving others.

Though my mother had a fine art degree, she could not find work outside of her factory job. She never complained, resented, or abandoned us. She found strength in providing for the children she did not imagine she'd have.

My father did technical writing for aircraft and satellite companies. He developed a waterproof housing for a movie camera and filmed underwater. He shot the Mayan ruins and collected ancient artifacts. He built and raced formula cars, bred tropical fish, did psychological experiments on coatimundi, covered boats with aircraft fabric, and did photography. He even had a career as a painter I did not learn about until after his death. He excelled at everything he tried without much apparent effort, and it all gave him nothing but momentary pleasure. He kept moving from place to place and from endeavor to endeavor chasing satisfaction. His insatiable wanderlust, and incurable curiosity, and need to escape himself kept him and us constantly moving. Other than when he was passed out drunk, he was never still.

The weight of his bitterness kept him from rising up to where my mother lived naturally, though he tried desperately to feel a moment of the purpose she embraced in her simple life. His doubt kept him from the faith and goodness she embodied. She was light, free from resentment, disappointment, and regret. His heart was full of dark pain. He could not comprehend the love she lived.

3

I forgave him for being unable to trust what he could not feel. I forgave her for not seeing who he really was under what he showed her. I appreciate it all—the dark, the light, the duality dance of life. I wonder how the two people who brought me into this world could be so different. Considering the utter contrast of my parents intrigues me as the duality dance of my life whirls around me.

Japanese Crane In Snow Field

2
Seed Settles On Sacred Soil

Seeds are designed to survive severe cold, extreme heat, drought, and infertile lands until finally, the conditions are right to germinate. Some cross oceans or are blown thousands of miles. Some are eaten by animals. Some lie dormant for years until the time is just right to bloom. Eventually, the fortunate seeds land on fertile soil and become magnificently what they were meant to be.

My mother knew it was necessary for me to stay in the sturdy shape until the time was right for me to blossom safely. My mother understood my tender shoots were too vulnerable, and petals too sensitive for this place. We knew there would be a time for me to flower, but until then, we accepted I had to stay contained in the protection of the seed shape, content to survive, waiting for the time to thrive.

The winds of chance cast my seed into the gale force of my father's destructive discontent. Staying in the calm eye of the storm of his rage required me to develop an ability to sense the subtle warnings of the violent turbulence brewing. Watching for the smallest changes of the brutal forces around me became a constant vigil. Staying precisely within the serenity of the very middle of the hurricane, within my seed shield, was required. This demanded alertness and agility to be ready to move quickly as the winds shifted. Staying silent to hear early warnings was my discipline: observing the slightest changes in the environment, my practice, and trusting my instincts—my way.

Occasionally, a kind visitor would come to see my mother when my siblings and father were not there, and only then would my mother say, "They are very nice, dear. Would you do your seed dance?" My mother wanted me to know there were some people who were gentle and among whom I could be safe. I would give my mother a small nod and then go into the other room. My mother would ask the guest to sit on the couch. When they were settled, I would come into the room and walk to the center. Sitting on my feet, I would fold the top of my body over the bottom, then tuck my head and curl my arms along my sides, putting my hands under my feet. After lying motionless in the seed shape for several minutes, I would begin to rise almost imperceptibly. First, my little arms, then torso, then legs would unfold like a sprout reaching for the light. Finally, when my whole body was upright, my arms would reach above my head. My small face would turn toward the sky. I would separate my arms as a flower in full bloom. Without any sound or movement, I would remain there for a few moments. Then I would bow toward the guest and leave the room silently. The visitors would be too stunned to utter a sound or applaud before I left the room. But this was as it should be. It was perfect because my seed dance was a gift, not a performance. When the dance was done, the gift had been given. Nothing more needed to happen, and everyone felt complete.

Mist & Mountain

3
Sleeper Wave Woke Me Up

There is a wave that comes without warning, from behind silently, without announcing its awesome force. The rogue wave knocked me down and carried me out to sea. They call it a sleeper wave, but it was really the wave that woke me up.

One moment I was tickling the spiky underside of a starfish, the next I was under a wall of turquoise. The surging waves tossed me like a button in a wild child's bathtub. Not being able to tell which way was up, I did not struggle or try to get there. The light came from everywhere. As it swirled around me, I was mesmerized. I did not think about breathing as I surrendered to the ocean. There was a strange comfort in being part of such immensity, and I was not afraid. Acceptance made me buoyant, and I floated up toward the sky. Not fighting allowed the currents to take me out into the sea before flowing parallel to the beach. Floating on my back with my tiny face at the surface, I took in air between wave surges splashing on my face. I had not been this far out before, but instead of fearing the distance from land, I felt a sense of freedom. Trusting the sea did not want to keep me forever, I relaxed and rose and fell with the waves like a seal playing in the surf.

My family and the other people on the beach were running back and forth looking for me. Some were screaming. Everybody except for my mother panicked. The fear of finding my limp body washed up lifeless and cold had overtaken most of them. Only my mother stayed calm as she kept repeating a chant softly toward the endless blue, "Please bring my daughter back to me. Please bring my daughter back to me." She understood that even if she could swim, the ocean was in charge. Only the sea could save me. The other people were frantically running in and out of the waves yelling as my mother knelt in the sand and kept whispering her plea.

Years later, she told me so much time had passed that they were certain I was gone. When they found me washed up on the shore like a tiny beached creature, I did not understand why she kept saying, "Thank you, thank you, thank you!" As she told the story of the day I was washed out to sea and washed back onto the beach unshaken, she said, laughing, "You only cried when we would not let you go back in the water."

She also told me, "You did not learn to swim; you just swam." And indeed, I don't remember ever not feeling at home in water. I do remember the seal dance I did on hot days in the backyard sprinkler wearing my cousin's hand-me-down black leotard.

All this came back to me vividly when my niece said, "You look like a Selkie," looking at photos a photographer had taken of me.

I said, "What is a Selkie?" She explained the Selkies are the dark Irish women who are really seals. They can come ashore and shed their skin to become human. If a man finds her seal skin, he then owns the Selkie unless she finds where her skin is hidden. Then she takes her seal skin and returns to the sea.

Perhaps what happened after sixteen years with my son's father was I came across where he tried to hide my true nature from me. For years I had been saying I felt he treated me like he owned me. So when I found my seal skin, I seized my freedom to explore the unknown depths of the seas of my own life, and my heart swam away.

Blue Lady Bird

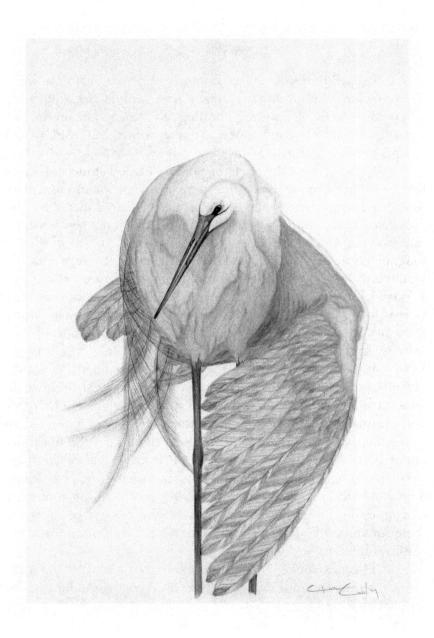

4
The Eye Of The Whale

I stood perfectly still in front of a porthole window while the rest of my family hurried to the next tank at the aquarium. They kept moving quickly, hoping to catch a glimpse of something wild. I stood alone, hoping something wild would catch a glimpse of me.

My face filled the circle of glass as I stood stone still at the first porthole window. It was the perfect height for me as a five-year-old. Hypnotized by the world of water I stared into, I felt the presence of something powerful, though I could not see anything but swaying light. Motionless, as if paralyzed, the feeling of a magnificence increased. If I could have made my legs move, I would have run, but the water's undulating light immobilized me. I looked into the softly swirling liquid for what seemed a long time before a whale's huge gray eye filled the window inches away from my small hazel eye. The whale was looking inside of me, into my mind, into my heart. Seeing this beautiful being trapped in this tiny tank, not roaming the oceans freely, filled me with a gigantic sadness. Tears pooled in my eyes, and I heard the whale speak to me inside of my being. It did not occur to me that this was unusual until I reflected on it much later when I wanted to remember what the whale said to me. At the time, I did not think about what the whale said. I simply felt it like waves of kindness passing through me and surrounding me all at the same time. The whale felt me, and I felt the whale, and that was enough. I had no desire to tell anyone. Whales see the interior of things as their sonar penetrates beneath the surface. They start from the truth we humans seldom reach.

This was one of those moments that changed my view forever, setting into motion an entirely different future than would have existed without the whale's eye filling the window and my heart. Its voice still surfaces within me. The whale still speaks to me. I can still feel the whale say, "You need not feel sadness for me. I am free because I feel. You do not need to be sad because you are free, because you feel. But your kind is not free, because they do not know what they feel. Feel for them. Feel compassion for them."

I still feel minuscule next to the whale's immense love, tiny next to the whale's gigantic wisdom. The whale filled me with compassion until there was no room left for anything else, even my name. When the guards found me, I could not remember who I was or how long I had been standing there alone, gazing into the mysteriously lit world. I could not even care about these things.

My father retold the story many times. "We went to the aquarium, and Clare did not want to be found, so she made up a last name."

Over the loudspeaker they heard, "There is a five-year-old girl at the front desk named Clare Jones."

The whale had filled me so full there was no room for anything unnecessary like a last name. Only the name my kind mother gave me remained. The guards wanted me to have a last name, so I picked one.

I do not remember what my father remembers. I only remember the whale.

Eye Of The Whale

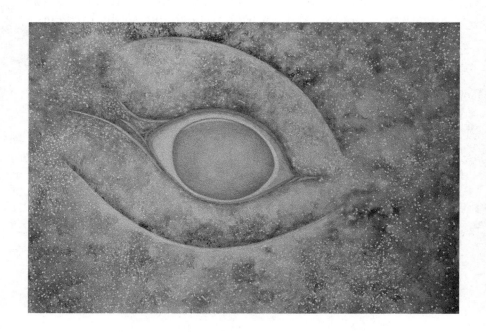

5
Sphere Of Serenity

Whenever I felt fear, I would imagine myself surrounded by a circle of light. I believed the dark was frightened by the light, and the light kept me shielded from danger. When uncertainty was around me, perhaps because I believed it would, the luminous sphere kept me safe.

Imagining floating around the world in a bubble lit from within was joyous. I counted on the freedom and safety I felt while envisioning the surrounding glow. When I drifted close to the sea's edge, the air in front of the wave would gently move me out of harm's way. I knew the wall of water would not crush me. I had no fear while I was in the radiant sphere. I felt protected from all danger.

Sometimes I rode the air currents, ascending like a bird out of deep canyons on warm thermals. In the circle of brilliance, I would soar above all concerns, and nothing could bother me. I often looked forward to going to bed so I could focus on the shining surrounding me and dream of traveling to distant places, far from the ordinary turmoil of home. I looked forward to bedtime when I could float away from all the loud sadness.

Within the light, I could breathe in the vacuum of space. When I looked back at earth from far, far away, I felt an all-encompassing peace.

While in the round radiance, I traveled to worlds where thoughts could be heard, so words need not be spoken. The more I visited those worlds, the more I could be comfortable in the world with others. I preferred my worlds where no one was unhappy, worlds where compassion was the queen everyone delighted in worshipping. In those gentle worlds, I could depend on everything being naturally beautiful. In my family home, nothing was predictable except for my mother's love.

There were times when keeping the light around me took tremendous effort. Other times, it surrounded me as if provided by some inexplicable, invisible force.

I did not try to understand how the surrounding light allowed me to survive the darkness. I simply trusted it, and it would be there when I needed it. The circle of light seemed to give me strength my siblings did not have. My younger sister coped with the chaos all around us by pretending everything was okay. She had to believe we were a normal family to carry on. After she was an adult, it became clear to her we were not normal, and I think it crushed her. She dropped out of the family entirely and has not returned. My aunt Jane said to me, "I do not understand why your little sister is not in your life. You were always kind to her." Perhaps that is why; she could not understand how I could be kind when so much around us was cruel.

My brother dealt with the unpredictable by staying in his bedroom, reading books. Maybe he needed to distract himself with a head full of facts to get through. My older sister numbed herself with all the drugs and alcohol she could find.

We all had our ways of coping. I retreated into quiet nature or into the circle of light. I returned refreshed and tried to create order in the chaos. I was third born and saw what did not work for my older sister and brother, so I tried something different that worked for me. Maybe my younger sister did not need to face the uncertainty because I watched over her and kept her safe.

When our father remarried, his new wife's daughter came into our lives. I took her under my wing and tried to give her a sense of security. I was the adult child watching over everyone. I became the authority even the adults turned to for direction.

My new sister said, "From my first memories of you when I was six years old, no matter what was going on, my mother, my grandmother, your father, brother or sisters, everybody turned to you for guidance."

I often remember walking into a room and sensing something was about to go wrong. I would quickly imagine the brilliant light surrounding the house while I determined who was about to lose control. Then I would do something to redirect the energy, blowing out the fuse before it reached the explosive hurt in their heart.

What everyone depended on me for was also a source of resentment. What some were appreciative of made others jealous. All I ever wanted was to bring everyone into the circle of light and keep them safe. I still do. The only thing that's changed is now I want to encircle the whole world in the luminous peace.

Monkey In The Moon

6
In God's House Nobody Was Home

My first-grade class vibrated with happy chaos like a garden painted by Van Gogh. My mother thought I may need more room to flower and took me to the big school on top of the hill. The new class was like a grove of trees planted in straight rows. The teacher waved her hand, signaling my mother and me to come to the back of the class. As we walked over, I noticed the children all kept their eyes down. She asked my mother questions. The only one I remember was, "Can your daughter read?"

My mother smiled with pride as she answered, "Not yet, but she tells wonderful stories while looking at the pictures."

The teacher showed my mother to the door and me to my seat, second in the first row. The teacher asked the girl in the first seat to stand up and read from the book on her desk. She stood slowly, appearing to have trouble getting her feet under her. Then she read one word and then the next, stopping and starting, straining, stumbling, and holding back tears. The teacher yelled, "Sit down." As she sat down, I could feel her body quivering through my desk. I was happy her turn was over without thinking I was next. When the teacher asked me to read, I felt like I was moving in slow motion as I stood thinking she must want me to tell a story. She could not possibly have forgotten so soon that my mother told her I could not read. As I swung my legs to put my feet under me, I glanced at a boy in the second row, and his kind eyes were smiling at me, which gave me courage. I looked at the picture in the book, and the words came effortlessly. The kids liked my story, so I continued until I heard the teacher shout, "What are you doing?"

Everyone froze as the teacher yelled at me, "Go to the front of the class." No one had ever yelled at me before. "Now!" she screamed. Paralyzed and confused, I could not believe this was happening. "I said now! Go to the front of the class and look at your classmates and tell them you lied." I do not remember walking from my desk to the front of the class. The class of frightened eyes looked at me kindly. She continued, "Tell them you cannot read. Tell them you are just a liar!"

Saying nothing, I stood there without moving until the lunch bell rang. As I walked out of the class and down the long corridor, it did not feel real. It felt like a nightmare. I found myself standing in the back of the gigantic empty church. They said it was God's house, so I waited motionless in the back of the church for God to come home. I heard the laughter of the kids on the playground outside. I listened without making a sound until the bell rang, and the laughter faded away, and everything went silent. My breath was the only sound I heard as I waited for God to come and talk to me. Maybe I was too small in the back of the huge church for God to see me, I thought. Peeling one foot off the floor and then the other, I took one tiny step then the next toward the front of the church. I wanted to give God time to get there before I reached the altar. The dead man with nails through his hands was terrifying. Feeling embarrassment for him being nearly naked, I kept looking at the floor. My tiny steps inched me forward. Eventually, I got to the line I did not want to cross and stopped. Perhaps God wants to be asked out loud, so I said in a soft voice, "Please talk to me!"

God did not come talk to me, and I could not bear the silence another moment, so I ran out of the church. Running until there was nothing but thick grass higher than my head all around me, I sat down. I felt a sadness I had not felt before, like I was not welcome in the world. It felt like I did not belong in this place. It was bright, but I did not feel the warmth of the sun. There was a breeze, but it did not soothe me. The grass swayed against my legs, but it did not tickle them as it used to. The clouds were dancing in the sky, and I could not care. Dragonflies tried to get my attention, and I ignored them. Ladybugs teased me, and I did not want to play. Nothing mattered because God didn't come talk to me. A tear slipped out of my eye, and I felt enormous anguish for the guy nailed to the cross. I could not accept he would be put there in front of everyone broken, bleeding, and undressed. I cried until I heard a voice that made no sound say, "You are not alone. You do not have to be with anyone who is not kind to you." I lay back in the embracing grass until the dismissal bell rang, and I walked home and said nothing.

The next day, I got dressed and left the house at the right time to go to school. Somewhere along the way, I slipped off the path and slipped between some bushes and off into a field where birds were busy making nests and caterpillars were inching up trees. I felt like I belonged there, and I was happy. On school days, I wandered into natural places along the way and did not end up at school. I kept busy and inspired by building little stone dams, branch bridges, seed mobiles, and feather pictures. I had projects and did not feel lonely. Talking with birds and watching clouds dance, I was at home in nature. Staying close enough to hear the children during recess on the playground was the perfect distance for me. At the end of the day, when the school bell rang, I would walk home before anyone else.

In the evenings when my family was all home, there was much commotion. I drew no attention to myself, and no one asked about school, nor did I mention how I spent my days. I simply slipped through the cracks the way liquid flows through any opening. My way was to find a peaceful place to replenish during the day to survive the unpredictable evenings. I did not drop out of school; I dropped into myself.

The Seekers

7
Under The Boat

My mother asked the next-door neighbor to check on us before she got home from work and my father got home from the bar. I would get home first. Minutes after I heard the school dismissal bell ring in the distance, I would run into the house to be alone for a few minutes in the bedroom I shared with my two sisters. The neighbor would call out as soon as she saw me go into my house, "What are you doing?"

I would yell out the window, "Cleaning my room," and she would let me be. Then I would take the old shoebox out from under my bed, opening my treasure chest with care equal to its precious contents. It was full of rough and shiny stones; round, oval, and wing-shaped seeds; white, pink, and orange seashells; and blue jay, crow, and sparrow feathers. Every day I would examine and admire each item as if it was the first time I saw it before adding something new. This daily ritual ended with me carefully closing the box to put it back under my bed, where no one ever looked.

Then the ritual would continue with me changing into one of the two hand-me-down black leotards I got from my cousins who took ballet. The box of nature's jewels, the two leotards, and a few normal clothes were my only possessions. Each day during my bath, I washed the leotard I wore while I danced in the backyard before anyone came home. The leotard would dry overnight, hung over the shower curtain, while the dry one from the day before was placed under my pillow. One day, the leotard I hung up the evening before was not on the shower curtain rod where I'd left it.

I put on the other one and went outside before anyone else came home as I did every day. The next-door neighbor was at her kitchen sink doing the dishes as I walked by. She looked at me like she saw a ghost and dropped what she was washing. I realized she didn't know I had two identical leotards, she must have come into the house and taken the one drying on the curtain rod. She could not figure out how I could be wearing it and could not contain her surprise. I think she just wanted me to fit in and be like the other girls and wear dresses. She looked scared, and I knew she had taken the leotard. I said nothing as usual and went to the backyard.

I had once played with her daughter, Trina, who kept dressing and undressing her dolls. They felt strange and smelled unpleasant. Their clothes were rough, busy patterns of bright colors that were not lovely to me. Trina always wore a cowgirl outfit with a holster and gun on each hip. She wanted me to play the Indian because I had dark hair. She wanted me to play dead when she shot me. I slipped away as soon as Trina's friend came in, and I did not play with her again.

I was comfortable being outside with the crickets and grasshoppers. It was not lonely for me to be alone. It seemed to me people were confused, and nature was not. People did not tell the truth, and nature never lied. In natural places, things felt real. Among people, things often felt false.

Every day Trina's brother would try to find me. Perhaps he wanted to see me dancing in the backyard. But the dances were not for him, so I made sure not to do them when he or anyone else was close by. When I heard him coming, I would hide beneath the upside-down fiberglass boat next to our house. There was a small cutout for the outboard motor, which appeared too small for anyone to squeeze through, so he never looked for me under the boat.

I loved the way the sun shining through the green fiberglass made the light so soft in my own little world. The pure white grass that grew under the boat was delicate and otherworldly. Everything in this world delighted me—the veins in leaves and the smell of the soil—all was serenely mysterious. Sometimes I would find albino worms and see-through bugs under the boat. I could lie there peacefully looking at the tiny creatures and plants for however long it took him to look everywhere except where I was. I would wait, knowing sometimes he would come back and check again, but not three times. He never found me, which made him angry, he would slam the gate behind him every day when he gave up looking and went to do something else.

When he was gone, I would come out on hot days to do a seal dance in the sprinklers. There was a different dance for every kind of light, every season, every creature, and every mood. I did not practice, repeat, or memorize them. They were natural and came without thought or hesitation, and I loved them all equally. They were meant for a particular moment and only that moment. The dances came like the sun comes to the morning, butterflies to flowers, frogs to puddles.

Toys, television, and comic books were not interesting to me. I only remember one toy from my childhood: a panda bear with a music box inside of it my aunt Jane gave me. I was fascinated by the music box, so I carefully opened the stuffed animal and removed it. I loved watching the tiny metal paddles hitting the spikes on the wheel, and I put the music box in with my other treasures.

Toys got broken, lost, taken, or my siblings would fight over them. I was glad I did not care about them. No one else valued my natural things, which filled me with wonder. What gave me comfort and inspiration caused no conflict, so I could have what I most cared about—peace in nature. While alone in natural places, I became part of whatever surrounded me. I danced with the gentle breeze to the sounds of the birds.

Pollinators

8
Satellite City's Sacred Service

Many times as a child, I dreamt of a place where all the people on earth lived. I called it Satellite City because the building stood so tall that it needed a satellite ring around the top to keep it from falling over. Everyone lived within the structure, leaving the earth uninhabited by humans. Each level of the structure was transparent with uninterrupted, spectacular views.

In the dream, I was often staring out, longing to be on the earth. I would imagine what I would need to bring along to survive out on the planet among the trees and creatures. The people around me in Satellite City seemed content. We all had everything we needed. But I yearned to smell moist soil after a rain or feel wet leaves under my feet. Part of me could recall the sensation of wind on my face even though my body had not felt it, as if my cells remembered something and longed for it.

I dreamt of this place often, and in each dream, I was someplace different within Satellite City. Sometimes I would dream I was outside the building walking on the earth.

While in the building, I was always looking out the windows. As I passed people, I could feel them wanting me to look at them. They would put their hands together and touch their fingertips to their forehead then to their hearts. I would do the same, and we would smile each time. Warmth came toward me from everyone in Satellite City. As soon as they passed, I would return to my contemplations of the land.

Everyone had a private area, and each family had a shared space. Most people ate in the beautiful large dining areas. In the dreams, I never saw myself eating there or speaking with anyone, but everyone acknowledged me as if they knew me.

Everyone's private area was respected, being the only place one could have solitude. The only time anyone ever came into another's private area was by invitation.

One night in my dream, I saw myself working as a sanctuary maid. No one ever went into anyone else's area when they were away except the sanctuary maid, so it was a most revered position. Only the most trusted ones would be allowed to enter into anyone's private space when they were not there. Though I dusted and vacuumed, my real duty was to clean out negativity, leaving pure light in its place.

Years later, as a young adult, I cleaned houses, often remembering my childhood dreams of Satellite City.

I enjoyed my work as a house cleaner. It was simple and peaceful and allowed me to think about art, my true work. I especially enjoyed cleaning for single working mothers. When I arrived, their homes felt heavy and messy. When I left, they felt light and organized. Now I have a big house and clean it myself. I enjoy cleaning before having events and recalling my Satellite City dreams. I thought what I enjoyed about cleaning was dancing through the house with inspirational music playing, but the ceremony of cleaning the space was actually more an opportunity to clear myself, to make myself porous and light, so everything passed through me. Once when I was unable to clean before an event in my home, all the guests' negativity found the darkness I had not cleared from my body and stuck to it. I was in pain for days.

Once at an exhibition of my paintings, a woman told me I looked familiar. She studied me for a long time then looked around the room at my paintings desperately searching for a clue. She said, "I know I have met you before."

I responded, "I have cleaned your house for over a year." Dressed elegantly and standing among my paintings, she could not imagine me as a house cleaner. Unlike in Satellite City, where people appreciated my services the most, here people are often confused, insecure, and pretentious. Most upsetting to her was my willingness to admit, in front of a group of admirers at my exhibition, that I cleaned houses.

I remembered then what I knew instinctively as a child, what the Aborigines know: the Dreamtime is the real time. In Satellite City, a maid was a position of high honor, as it should be. I am filled with a sense of great appreciation whenever I recall the sweet eyes of the people in Satellite City, acknowledging my sacred service.

Bird Lines

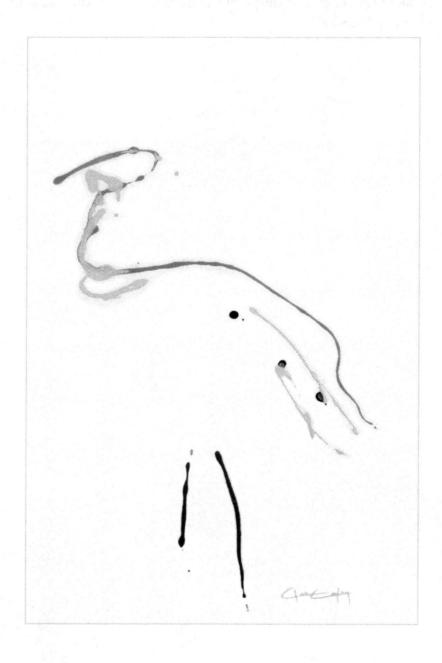

9
Saints And Snowflakes In Salina

When we left San Diego for Salina, Kansas, I did not know why. I imagine my father's desire to escape himself was the reason we moved so often. Perhaps the sense of leaving everything behind comforted him. His constant urge to get away from his present reality seemed to be temporarily satisfied while moving at sixty-five miles per hour. He loved to drive long stretches without stopping and had an enormous capacity for it. I think while moving, he experienced a state as close to peace as he could. As we crossed Arizona, New Mexico, and Texas, my father was almost serene.

Often the six of us would pile into the car at dawn, and my father would not stop driving until he was on the razor's edge of unconsciousness. At precisely noon, his daily ritual began with opening a beer, which was replaced by another, and then another, so his left hand was not without a beer until he passed out. There were times he kept driving until he realized he was hallucinating, there were other times, he did not know that what he was seeing was not actually there. I remember him driving until the early hours of the morning and saying, "Let's sleep in this grove of trees."

I said, "Good idea," even though there was not a single tree in any direction.

Road trips could be surreal ordeals. My mother and I would silently work together. Sometimes she would see danger I did not and with one glance give me information that could not be voiced. I was the one in the family who could navigate the minefield of my father's rage without stepping on a landmine. My mother would set markers to warn me where his explosives were buried. We were spies behind enemy lines. We learned a way to communicate secret messages so they would not be intercepted.

During the day, my father was still sober enough to navigate safely, but his focus and reaction time were dangerously impaired by nightfall. I knew I had to stay awake until he would

31

pull over to sleep, no matter how long it took. I would nap as much as possible when everyone else was awake, conserving my energy so I could endure the long nights. The later the night, the more likely he was to wander into oncoming traffic or off the shoulder. I could not say, "Dad, you're drunk. Pull over," because that would ignite his explosive anger. My father had his own bizarre code allowing him to whip his son, verbally abuse his oldest daughter, ridicule his youngest daughter, and call his kind wife a suffering Christian martyr. But, for whatever reason, he did not demean or strike me. Perhaps I escaped his wrath because I stayed silent. I did not challenge him because I figured out he could not tolerate criticism, being held accountable, or being wrong.

When we got to Salina, the sky was the color of dust. My father parked our metal home on wheels in a trailer park surrounded by hog farms. There was nothing green in the park to slow down the icy winds across the flat terrain. When frost came to Salina, I had no place to disappear outside, and there was no place to hide in our forty-foot trailer, so I had to go to school. Because I was the most foreign-looking girl in the Kansas Catholic school, I think that was why the teacher picked me to play Our Lady of Guadalupe in the class play. Being too shy to speak only made me more fit for the part. This was the only thing I ever participated in during elementary school. When I told my mother about it, she showed me a painting of Our Lady of Guadalupe in a seed-shaped circle of light. I imagined everyone traveled around the world in their minds in a bubble of light. I felt an inexplicable connection to this blessed vision. It did not feel miraculous; it felt matter of fact.

What did appear miraculous that winter took place outside our trailer one cold morning. On a piece of jet black tar paper laying on the ground, one after another, tiny miracles showed up. They were each sparkling perfection; an iridescent shimmer of frozen grace stunned me with its beauty. I examined every delicate thread, every minute point of the brilliant symmetry. As each snowflake appeared, I studied it closely, and indeed it was different from the one before. As another settled on the tar paper and then another, my mind raced, trying to memorize each shape as they fell faster and faster. I tried

32

desperately to match one to another while lying on my belly inches from the minuscule jewels.

As the blackness was slowly covered with glistening whiteness, I tried to imagine how many different snowflakes there must have been. How many were falling that morning in just that place? Then I thought about how many snowflakes must fall in all the other places and how each one was different. I could not hold the immensity of this in my mind. I lost all sense of cold and time. I was transported by the simple snowflakes' beauty and hoped Our Lady of Guadalupe could see them too.

Bird Of Paradise In Black Glass

10
Speaking Rock's Unspoken Secret

On the drive up the dirt road to the Canyon de Chelly overlook, my father told us the Navajo legend about Spider-Woman. He began with, "Speaking Rock tells Spider-Woman when a child is bad, and then Spider-Woman comes down off her high rock and takes the bad child to the top of Spider Rock where she devours them." Then he pointed out the car window to the top of the monolithic stone and said, "See the white at the top of Spider Rock? That is the bad children's bones, bleached by the sun." He looked at my older sister and said, "Spider-Woman will certainly feast on your fat body." My father seldom passed up an opportunity to frighten or insult. Though I did not know what devour meant, I knew it was not good. I barely spoke, sensing it was safer not to let my father know how I thought.

As soon as the crackling of the gravel beneath the jeep tires stopped, I ran as fast as I could through the clearing dust to the cliff's edge. There, standing up from the valley floor were the two towers of stone, Speaking and Spider Rocks. The spires were so tall and narrow they appeared to be built by whimsical gods. The scale of their beauty made everything else small. The herd of sheep in the valley below was a ball of lint blowing along a thin blue thread river. The Navajo sheepherder on his horse a tiny speck of gray with his cotton ball herd of sheep. Entranced by the scale, I wondered if the Navajo sheepherder told his children the same story my father told us. Perhaps the sheepherder heard the story I was hearing whispered on the wind —Speaking Rock's secret. Those who listen with their hearts hear different stories, soft utterances of nature, words on wind, rustling of dry leaves, water over rocks, lizards scurrying across hot sand, or crickets rubbing their legs together.

I heard Speaking Rock say, "There are no bad children, only sad children." Speaking Rock knows this, it stands so high it can see everything, even the inside of things. It can see into the children's hearts. It sees the hurt cause them to be sad and act badly. Speaking Rock tells Spider-Woman which children are sad. Then Spider-Woman climbs down and takes the unfortunate ones up to the top of her high rock. There the children have Spider-Woman's many other children to play with, and they are happy again. Up there, the air is so pure it makes them giddy. Up there, the birds teach them how to grow their own beautiful wings. The story I heard was that the white at the top of the high rock was their lovely feathers.

My trance was broken by my brother's quivering voice pleading, "Clare, sit down!" He was lying on his belly in the dirt behind me. I turned to look at him, and he looked terrified as he gestured with one hand for me to sit down. I thought our father's story must have scared him. I stepped closer to my brother, and he spoke sternly, "One gust of wind could have blown you over the edge to your death! You had your toes hanging over the edge! What were you thinking?"

My father was leaning on the hood of the car with his customary beer in his left hand, and yelled, "She thinks she can fly!"

Turning to look back at Canyon de Chelly, I whispered, "Thank you for telling me Speaking Rock's unspoken secret.

Momma Bird

11
Foot In The Fire

Solitary moments in serene nature are the most vivid memories of my childhood. I remember things like glistening snail trails of silver on smooth, dark bark, the gentle quivering of iridescent butterfly wings, glowing salamander bellies, rainbows undulating on dewdrops, and light dancing across the water. Finding natural materials that inspired me was my daily quest. With them, I could create anything I could imagine, and I could imagine so much when there were no distractions by loud and large people. I built bridges out of sticks, tiny pine needle baskets, seashell mobiles, stone labyrinths, feather masks, and moss clothing.

My father's all-pervasive need to get away from himself kept us moving from place to place. But I could always find somewhere to explore and be happy until we we stopped in Orange County. The strain of pulling a forty-foot trailer home from San Diego to Salina, Kansas, then to Spokane, Washington, then back to California was too much for the transmission of the Toyota Land Cruiser. As we were passing through Orange County on the way to Mexico, with one enormous snap, everything changed. My father put our trailer in a park one block from Disneyland. Nothing was real or beautiful to me there. Even the Matterhorn mountain was artificial. I could not find anything pure. Even the orange groves were planted in straight, strange rows. Being surrounded by stuff used only to entertain people looking for distractions from themselves made me sad. There was nothing there I felt any connection to. So much surrounded us, and I felt disconnected from it. All the electric lights and fireworks did not illuminate the darkness in my heart. Being constantly surrounded by other people did not alleviate my feeling of loneliness. I could not find nature to retreat into, and I began to feel despair.

The trailer park manager evicted us, saying we were an eyesore as my father's used sports car collection grew. We were the only ones with such things in this manicured land. He bought us a house where all the houses looked the same except for their paint colors with strange names. Nothing was wild. Even the plants and lawns were tame.

We moved in before the utilities had been turned on in the house, and it was unusually cold for Southern California. For heat, my father lit charcoal in a hibachi, and he put it in the room where he and my asthmatic mother slept with all the windows closed.

I listened to every tiny sound long after everyone had fallen asleep, sensing something was terribly wrong. Not knowing what it was, I stared into the darkness, looking for a sign of the danger I felt gathering around us. I lay perfectly still as my father got up and took his sleeping bag into the living room. A very clear and insistent voice within me said, "Do not go to sleep!" The desire to sleep kept increasing, and the voice kept getting stronger, "Do not go to sleep!" I tried to focus on the doorway two feet in front of me, but when I realized I could not, terror came over me, and the voice said, "Stand up!" I could not feel my legs. I threw the blanket off and stared at my feet. I felt no connection to my own body. I tried to get my feet to move.

I had the thought, I am dying! We are all dying. It was like an electric shock, and I stood up and vomited, which cleared my head. I somehow knew my mother was in a life-threatening situation. I struggled to feel my way down the hall to the room where she was sleeping. I did not know whether I was actually speaking or imagining I was speaking. "Wake up! We have to get out!" She did not move. Looking down, I saw my right foot was in the red-hot coals in the hibachi, and it shocked me into speaking clearly. "My foot is in the fire, and I can't feel it." She looked over and leaped out of her bed, shaking her head like a mother bear waking from hibernation. She picked me up and out of the coals. Moving in slow motion, we helped each other out of the room, groping and stumbling.

We woke up my big sister, who ran around the house in a frenzy, throwing everything she could pick up out into the backyard. I could not wake up or pick up my younger sister, so I dragged her down the hall into the living room. Instinctively, I opened every door and window in the house. My mother told my older sister to call 911. My younger sister still did not wake up, so I hauled her out onto the front lawn. My father sat up and started cursing under his breath. I went and tried to wake my brother. My father came in and started kicking him in a rage. I got between them, and my father left the room yelling obscenities. My brother then crawled out to the lawn with the rest of us. When the ambulance arrived, my younger sister was still unconscious, so they took her to the hospital, where they said she had carbon monoxide poisoning from the charcoal.

Many people said my father was a genius. He had several college degrees and had done technical writing for engineers, so how could he have not known about the poisonous gas replacing the oxygen in the house as the coals in the hibachi burned? Why did he take his sleeping bag to the living room and close my mother's bedroom door? There is so much in life we will never know.

We all slept on the front lawn that night. Every time I moved my head, I vomited and felt a little better until I could finally sleep.

At first light, my mother and I woke simultaneously, looking at each other, I remembered my right foot in the red-hot coals. I took it out of my sleeping bag, and we both saw ash still on it, but no burns. As usual, we smiled at each other when no one else was looking, knowing our bond could upset them. With a small nod, we silently acknowledged this and the mysterious benevolent forces we felt watching over us. I wondered if there were no burns because I only imagined the coals were still red hot or because something mysterious was watching over me when I put my foot in the fire.

Sarus Cranes Mating Dance

12
Why Pygmies Can't Go To Heaven

On one very unusual day, I became curious where the kids in the neighborhood were going, so I joined the group shuffling down the sidewalk. No one noticed because they were all talking at the same time. Following quietly behind, I flowed along as they went into a trailer next to an elementary school. I sat in a seat behind the tallest boy. Inside, the trailer had fake wood wallpaper, fluorescent lights, lots of posters of Jesus, and one of the Virgin Mother Mary.

The woman at the front of the trailer wore nylons that came just below her knees and a dark blue dress that landed just above her knees. She looked out the window as she said, "The Bible is the word of God."

A boy with a grown man's jacket said enthusiastically, "God wrote the Bible?"

She looked annoyed. "No, God didn't write it." I wanted to ask how she knew it was God's words if God did not write it, but did not dare. She continued responding to the boy, saying, "Men wrote down God's words." She held up the book and fanned the pages toward us. I wondered why the paper was so thin and the writing so small. I had lots of questions. How did they hear God's words? How did they know it was God? Did they see God when they heard his words? What did God look like? How did they know God was a man? How did they know it was really God, not just some other man? Did any women hear God's words?

I did not ask any of my many questions, even though what she read of God's words did not make sense to me. I thought God must be smart and able to speak in a way we can understand. Maybe it was because the men who wrote the Bible didn't have very good handwriting. Maybe girls should have written the Bible because they usually have better handwriting. I didn't say anything because she was not nice to anyone who did say something.

Nobody was listening, but there was a girl with braids who pretended she cared whenever the instructor looked in her direction. The others stared at their shoes, twirled their hair, bounced in their seats, doodled, and tapped their pencils on the desks.

I wanted God's words to make sense to me, so I kept listening. I was the only one who seemed to be listening until she mentioned hell, which got everyone's attention. She got very lively as she said, "Hell is for sinners. It's burning hot, and you have to work all the time, digging and breaking rocks and carrying heavy things. There's no food or water in hell. Sinners never get to rest, and they have to stay in hell forever. She went on and on about the horrors of hell, which she seemed to know a lot about!

She continued, "Heaven is for the good people who have been baptized in the name of the Lord."

She didn't describe heaven, so the girl with braids asked, "What's heaven like?"

The teacher did not like any questions and snapped as she replied, "Heaven is paradise. But you only get to go there if you don't commit any mortal sins, and you're baptized in the name of Jesus."

That made me think about the Pygmies deep in the jungle who never heard of Jesus. I loved hearing stories about them and remembered hearing how they settled family disputes. The elders of the tribes, who watched over the children while the men and women were out looking for food, would dismantle the hut of the quarreling couple. When the couple would return, they would have to cooperate to get their hut up before nightfall. I thought, what a lovely idea. It made sense to me. The Pygmies seemed so gentle and kind to one another. It upset me to think they could not go to paradise just because they lived in the jungle and never heard of Jesus. So I mustered up the courage to raise my hand and ask, "What if a Pygmy was good to everybody and never sinned? Shouldn't they go to heaven?"

"They would go to purgatory," she barked.

"What's purgatory?" I asked.

"It's not heaven, it's not hell. It's someplace in between."

43

I was very confused and said, "But if the Pygmies had always been nice, then they should go to heaven."

"I already said they go to purgatory. Heaven is for the baptized," she snapped.

I burst out, "But that is not fair, and God must be fair."

The teacher swung around, pointed to the door, and yelled, "You have no right to say what is fair or what God should do. Leave!"

While walking home, I thought maybe the writing in the book was too small for her to read. Maybe she just pretended to understand the Bible. Perhaps the men who wrote it did not really hear the words of God. It was clear to me whomever God was, she or he or they must be kind. I felt certain the word of God was there for everybody to hear inside. I thought the teacher had not heard the voice of God inside herself. She was confused, thinking God was somewhere else. I felt sorry for her. I said a little blessing for her to be able to hear the truth inside herself someday, and I did not feel sad anymore.

Three Wise Birds

13
Crazy Carrot

Something about their identical suits approaching my front door was disturbing. Even from my fourteen-year-old inexperienced perspective, I knew this was going to change things. Never having seen such serious-looking men up close before, these truancy officers both intrigued and terrified me. As soon as I opened the door, the shorter one asked, "Are you Clare Cooley?"

"I am," I answered.

The taller one snapped in a stern tone, "Why aren't you in school?"

I answered without hesitation, "Who will take care of things?"

"What do you mean?" He asked, clearly puzzled.

"My father is gone. My asthmatic mother works twelve-hour shifts six days a week in a punch press factory and is too tired to shop, cook, clean, or do laundry, so I do."

The shorter man's eyes began to form tears, the taller man took him by the upper arm and pulled him back while saying to me, "We'll get back to you."

I had been slipping through the openings since I was seven years old. The path of least resistance was to simply step off the sidewalk on the way to school. I would find serene nature to be my classroom. I headed out before anyone else every day. We had moved six times and gone to seven different schools by then. Maybe I was just lost in the chaos, or perhaps my father and oldest sibling were so angry and loud, they did not care to have any other Cooley in their school. I cannot explain how no one noticed or showed up until I was fourteen. But now that I'd been noticed, things would be different.

After a series of meetings weeks after the truancy officers came to the front door, it was decided by the board of education that my mother should take me to a psychiatrist. It did not make sense to me, but I agreed to go without resistance. I understood that my mother could get in trouble because I had not been going to school. She was already suffering, realizing for the first time how little school I had attended. I never blamed her for not knowing, as I had perfected the art of drawing no attention to myself, and she had so many more pressing concerns to deal with. There were no calm moments in our home for my mother to even ask, "How's school?" Between moving so often, my father's drunken rages, my older sister's dangerous drug use and her threatening friends, my older brother's depression, my little sister's emotional vulnerability, and my mother's asthma, my truancy was easy to overlook. I got dressed and packed my lunch every school day. Everyone knew I liked to be alone, so leaving before my siblings and coming home first raised no suspicion. I acted as if everything was fine, because after a day in the serenity of solitude in nature, I was calm and happy. My way of finding a safe place in an exhausting and dangerous world refreshed me.

I was surprised that the board of education required me to go to a psychiatrist. My mother drove me there and waited in the car as I went into the office, where a jumpy receptionist led me into the doctor's office. He was a large-framed man with a thick silver and black mustache, sitting behind an enormous desk. The psychiatrist pointed to a big couch across the room, gesturing for me to sit. It was soft leather, and I sank into it and felt tiny. He greeted me politely, which seemed reasonable, but then immediately said, "Do you know how psychic you are?"

I withheld any show of surprise while I tried to figure out how to respond. Before I came up with anything, he continued, "What am I writing down?" My first thought was, what kind of a trick is this? He had a yellow legal pad he held straight up and down in front of his chest and scribbled something onto it without me being able to see his hand or pencil. Then he put the pad a few inches in front of his chest flat against himself. He held it there with his left arm and looked at me without saying anything. I was trying to imagine what he was up to. How do I appear cooperative? As I reviewed my possible responses carefully, considering the negative repercussions for my mother if I did not cooperate, I knew I must go along with him.

Just then, the receptionist tapped on the door and came in, saying, "Sorry to interrupt, but Mrs. Miller is on line one and very upset." I thought perhaps he was going to set the pad down while speaking with a make-believe disturbed client. Perhaps he would let its reflection flash in the picture glass behind him, or maybe there would be a faint trace of graphite on his white shirt. I thought one way or another he's going to reveal what he has put on the paper. My best guess was it was a test of my perceptive abilities, alertness, or honesty.

Abruptly, but politely, he said to Mrs. Miller, "We will talk about it during your next session. Goodbye." He hung up and looked directly at me. He had not taken the pad away from his shirt, so there was no way for me to see any reflection. I could not see how his pencil moved as he held his hand completely behind the pad, nor could I see the shape or pattern it moved in when he wrote.

I was very confused by it all and at a loss of how to respond. Sensing my discomfort, he said, "This is for you. What have I written down?"

I felt very uncomfortable. With no desire to be right, I just wanted it to be over. I said the first thing that came into my mind, "A carrot." He turned his pad over and showed me a small, simple outline in the center of the page of a carrot with a leafy top. He showed no reaction and appeared unimpressed. I felt a little panicked and began searching for an explanation. I ruled out every possibility of him telegraphing the answer to me somehow, clues in his phone call, his secretary. There was no carrot art, bunnies, or Easter baskets in the waiting room. No smell of carrots, not even orange colors. If it was a trick, he had tricked me, which was mildly disturbing. But what made my heart race was the terrifying idea it was not a trick—the idea he actually knew something about me. He broke my silence by asking, "Why don't you wear shoes?"

"They are uncomfortable."

"Why haven't you been going to school?"

"I feel the need to help my mother with managing the house and prefer being alone."

"Why?"

"Alone, I can relax."

"Why can't you relax in school?"

"I don't fit in."

"Why do you think you don't fit in?"

"Because I don't."

"I would appreciate it if you would try to explain."

"Girls my age are talking about matching their nail polish to their shoes, while I'm thinking about feeding the five of us on the twelve dollars a week left over for food after critical bills are paid."

"Tell me more about your situation, if you don't mind."

"My mother has a fine art education and has had severe asthma since her infancy. To support us, she works on a punch press in a factory and comes home every day unable to turn her head because of muscle strain. My dad is an overqualified, underemployed alcoholic who is gone now, thank goodness because he is violent! My older sister is always looking for bad drugs. If my brother is home, he is in his room reading. My little sister lives in a make-believe world where she must believe we are normal. And I cannot stand to live in squalor, so I do all the cleaning, shopping, cooking, and laundry."

He looked into my eyes for a long time, and I noticed I did not mind, so I asked, "Am I crazy?"

"Oh, no!"

"So, will I fit in?"

"Definitely not."

"Why?"

"Because the world is crazy, and you are not."

I was somewhat sad about not fitting in, but what ripped my heart wide open was hearing him say what I also believed was true—the world was crazy. I came into his office with my shields up, but I left surprised I trusted this stranger I was forced to see. As I got in the car where my mother was waiting, she asked, "Was it okay, dear?"

"Fine. He's nice." My answer surprised us both.

Late that night, my mother answered the phone and handed it to me, saying, "It's the doctor, dear."

"Hello," he said. "I hope I am not calling too late. I just wanted to thank you for coming in today. You uplifted me. Most people complain about nothing. You have so much to complain about, but you don't. When you left, I felt better than when you

49

walked in, which never happens." After a short silence, he added, "Don't change. Don't let them change you!"

My mother's round, dark eyes were studying me as I said, "Thank you. I enjoyed meeting you too. Good night, Doctor." My mother smiled and went back to her sewing project without a word about the call. I saw the doctor for about a year, and we talked of many things, but not ever again about carrots or being crazy.

Egret On Branch

14
When The Goddess Looked Away

Everything is normal. My father is passed out drunk, my mother is at the factory working, my older sister is looking for drugs, my brother is in his room reading, my younger sister is pretending everything is fine. I'm laying on the living room floor looking at an oceanic picture book transported by the strange beauty of creatures that live deep in the sea.

Whenever I cannot be in nature, I imagine myself someplace natural, where everything is dignified, even death. Dwelling in these realms, I do not feel lonely. Dreaming of cranes, waterfalls, sunsets, space, and the sea, I am free and happy. As I look at photographs of creatures living in the lightless depths, I am fascinated by their unusual elegance. To me, everything in nature is beautiful. I see loveliness even in the ones who frighten me, like the fish with a single light at the end of a long bobbing spine protruding from its head, a light not meant to illuminate its way through the dark but to lure in prey.

A knock at the door shatters my deep-water trance. My connection to these ancient ones evaporates as I open the door to one of my father's barroom buddies. His baby face does not fit atop his massive construction worker's frame. He looks uncomfortable and unnatural, like a child trapped in a man's body. I feel compassion for him. He asks for my father while fidgeting with his buttons. My hand twitches, wanting to close the door, but my mind says, let him in. He can wake my father from his intoxicated slumber before my mother comes home and discovers him there. I do not want my mother to find her ex-husband there two years after their divorce! Reluctantly, I open the door without speaking and go back to my book on the floor. He does not wake my father but lies on the floor next to me. I squirm sideways across the synthetic carpet, burning my knees to get further from him. He wraps his vise grip hand around my tiny twig arm. His huge body turns my little body over effortlessly. In the next instant, he is lying on top of me. I can't breathe as I feel the pressure of his oversized body crushing my small frame like being pushed to the bottom of the sea. Every muscle in my body strains, but I cannot move in any direction. I feel panic for the first time in my life. In one of his massive hands he puts both my wrists over my head and reaches down with his other hand moving my shorts and underwear out of the way. I feel my ribs will snap as he puts all of his weight on my chest. I want to disappear, die, or just cease to exist. I scream silently as he wedges his thick legs between mine. I did not know why, but I knew I should not wake my father. Many years later, I came to understand why I knew he was not safe. My spirit left my body I could not bear to be in anymore. It was not the physical pain I could not bear; it was the humiliation. I had not kissed or held hands with a boy. I did not go to school, watch television, read, see movies, or have conversations. Though I had never been spanked or forced to do anything before this, and I had no word for what was happening to me, I understood it was wrong—very, very wrong.

Looking down from above, my spirit spoke to my empty shell body. "He can only hurt your body; he cannot touch you where you really live. Your sacredness is out of his reach. He wants your goodness, but he cannot take it. No matter what happens, do not give your goodness away! Promise you will never give your goodness away!"

He tried to force himself into my tiny body with a couple of thrusts and then collapsed. I focused all my attention on making the silent promise, "I will not let him take my goodness!"

When I snapped back into my body I felt a wet heat between my legs, tears burst from my eyes. He pulled back, looking at me as if waking from a nightmare. Horror twisted his baby face into a hideous shape. He jumped up and ran out, leaving the front door wide open.

I went to the empty bedroom and hid behind a pile of dirty clothes in the lightless corner of the closet. Without uttering a sound, I wept tears from the center of my being, from the core of the earth itself. For the first time in my life, I could not bear to be alive. I wanted to leave it all behind. It was not the horror of what the baby-faced monster did to me I could not bear; it was living in a world without protection. I did not want to be in a

53

world where no one was safe. I did not want to live in a world without beauty and grace, a world where people could take something not offered to them. Understanding there was a world I never imagined existed, a world of betrayal, was more than I wanted to bear.

Minutes later, I heard my father closing the wide-open front door behind him. I went to the shower and tried to wash off the feeling of filth, but I could not. I knew soon my mother would be home from work exhausted, and for her I had to bear the unbearable secret and withhold all that had happened while she was away. I feared if I told her, she might kill my father or his barroom buddy, and she might go to jail, or she would be too sad to bear it. So I thought I had to keep the terrible secret to protect her.

I wept in the shower until it ran cold, pleading, "Tell me someone watches over me. Please tell me what just happened was only in an instant when the goddess looked away."

An Opening In Space

15
Bridge To The Other Side

I walked whenever despair came over me. While walking, I never decided beforehand which way to go, which made me feel safer. Bad men could not predict my movements if I stayed spontaneous, I thought. Free flowing became a way of life—my way to survive. Choosing direction by following the scent of jasmine, a warm breeze. Letting a root growing under the sidewalk cause one shoulder to dip and my body to lean, discovering paths. My daily journey strengthened my connection to intuition and instincts.

Often I would end up at the same freeway overpass. Walking to the center of the bridge, I would stop and look down. My mind would fill with a sense of relief with the thought of letting go. I would imagine myself falling through space. It was intoxicating envisioning myself as a small bird drifting on warm currents or a leaf suspended on a gentle breeze. I was happy in those weightless moments, free from gravity, free from harm, free from all earthly concerns.

Walking to the center of the bridge, I would stop and stare down. The car lights were like phosphorescent fish, swimming in schools, shimmering luminescence soothing me. The little car schools of fish scurried away from the big truck sharks.

I would see myself leaping over the edge, over the edge of suffering, over the edge of surrender, over the edge of uncertainty, over the edge of life. I would drift down, losing all heaviness, separation, and desire. Drifting down, I would join the freeway sea and become part of something again.

Grace had always surrounded me before this time. Simple things had delighted me. My world had been one where I could find beauty everywhere. Now I could not find natural beauty anywhere. Everything was artificial, without purpose.

My longing for death wasn't because of carrying the baby-faced monster's child within me. It wasn't knowing I would never hold this child. It was not this making me desire death. It was the shame of being human making me want to let go. Shame for being born among those who hurt others for pleasure is what made me want to leave everything behind and enter the unknown, the void, and become part of the mystery again.

One cool afternoon, I stood on the freeway overpass for so long the sky got completely dark. Watching the schools of freeway fish, I lost all sense of myself. I could not feel my hands on the cold steel rail. The endless stream of traffic made me dizzy. It would be so easy to cross the bridge to the other side. Letting go would be so effortless. Not letting go took all my strength. I was so tired of hanging on, and at that moment, I could not think of any reason to. Maybe I would come back as something I could respect—not a human, a crane perhaps. Or I could just turn into light, and no one could ever hurt me again.

Then the meaning of my name came into my mind, clear bright light, and my trance of despair broke as I thought about my mother giving me my name. Then I thought how will she go on without me? What about the innocent and unborn child in my womb who deserves only love? Thinking of others gave me gravity again. The night air on my face felt good. Breathing deep into my lungs, my hands let go of the cold metal railing. In the midst of tremendous pain, I considered others. My blood surged with warmth as I turned away from despair, toward love as I walked across the bridge to the other side.

Flamingos And Magnolias

16
Forgiveness Is The Best Revenge

My childhood ended the evening the baby-faced monster came through the door. I became a two-thousand-year-old woman in a sixteen-year-old body. Though I did not have a word for what happened to me, I knew it wasn't right.

Immediately I felt life reach its kindling point within me. I was carrying a stranger's child forced into me. It was clear I could not keep either of us safe. I understood I would not get to see my child sleep, learn to walk, catch a ball, or ride a bike. Nor would my child get to know his mother's face, voice, or scent. For his safety, I had to let adults raise him. I hurt too much to cry. I feared there would be no end to the tears. I believed I had to contain the pain to be brave enough to do what I had to for my baby.

A few days after my baby was born, he was adopted by a couple who could protect him. I walked across town to a dark bar where my father drank. He was lonely, and I felt sorry for him. Whenever I went to see him, he would stop drinking for a while. It made me feel better to help someone else, and I loved him even though I didn't trust him. He was my father, and I wanted to help.

He would leave the Red Lion bar when I came to see him, knowing I hated everything about it: the smell of beer, cigarettes, sweaty men, cheap perfume, rancid oil on the popcorn, the noise of the TV, the jukebox, the pinball machine, and everyone talking at once while no one was listening. Nothing was lovely or natural there. No windows, only artificial light. Most days I waited outside the musty bar. This particular day, I was waiting inside so my father would not order another beer before he finished his pool game.

I did not ever speak or look into anyone's eyes in the bar. I did not turn around to see who sat behind me. I heard a voice say, "Why didn't you tell me? I would have married you."

Until then, I had partly blamed myself for what happened. Saying things to myself like, "I should not have said hello the night he was at the Mexican Bar when I picked up my father," "I shouldn't have opened the door," "I shouldn't have thought I was safe just because my father was there," "I shouldn't have worn shorts," "I shouldn't have gone back to my book on the living room floor," "I should have screamed even though I couldn't," "I should have hit him even though I couldn't," or "I should have known something I never knew existed was about to happen to me."

But now, hearing the baby-faced monster's voice again, I did not blame myself anymore. Instead, I was filled with disgust. I wanted to be outraged. I wished I wanted to hurt him, to pick up the bar stool and hit him over the head, or grab my father's pool cue and run it through his heart, or take the tequila bottle and break it on his nose, or scream at the top of my lungs, "You raped me and left the state that night. You got married within a week and returned after I endured arranging for my child to be adopted, and now you act like we had an affair?" I wished I wanted to hurt him as he hurt me, but I could not feel anything but pity for him. All this flashed through my mind in an instant. I should want revenge. I should want him to suffer. I should yell loud enough for everyone to hear, "You are just what every young lady dreams of for a husband—a rapist! Who is this charade for? My father or your guilty conscience? We did not have an affair! You forced yourself on me and left a child within me that could not be raised by his mother!"

I wished I wanted to humiliate him, but if I let myself be filled with hate, I would be like him. So I got up and walked out without looking back. As soon as I was outside, I started to run in the opposite direction of home so no one could predict my path. I hid behind some industrial buildings for a while before I began walking a meandering route down strange little streets. Whenever a car came turning onto the block, I disappeared behind bushes until it was gone.

On a tiny street where no one seemed to be home, I stopped and sat under a ginkgo tree. The tiny fan leaves sprinkled on the ground were so lovely that their grace made me cry. The first tears came softly, and then they flowed like a wild mountain river in the spring thaw, rushing out of my eyes, over my cheeks, across the lawn and the yellow flowers growing up through the cracks in the sidewalk. A river of tears poured off my mountain of silence until my eyes were so clean I could see clearly.

I could see he could rape me, but he could not take my dignity. I could see he could take my childhood, but he could not take my innocence. I could see my innocence was not lost— just hidden. I had buried it deep in my own heart like people burying the family jewels as the enemy approaches. I started digging frantically inside of myself, leaving holes everywhere looking for it. Still, I could not find the brilliant gems of innocence. My internal struggle was trying to understand what had happened to me and why it had destroyed the landmarks to guide me back. I cried and whispered, "Please help me find my innocence."

I heard a tender voice surface from my own depths, saying, "The map is in your heart." I looked in my heart and found directions. "Go over the mountains of hurt, cross over the rivers of rage, pass through the forests of fear, and you will find your innocence there."

"But how will I find my way?"

"By staying on the path."

"What is the path?"

"The path is forgiveness."

"How can I forgive a man who raped me, who ended my childhood in one selfish, cruel moment?"

"He tried to steal your innocence because he could not find his own after someone tried to steal it from him."

Then, a vision of him as a four-year-old child came into my mind. I saw my father was once innocent, open, and trusting. My older sister, and everyone who had ever hurt me, were lost on the way back to their own innocence. I could see back to the beginning of innocence, back to the beginning of fear, the beginning of pain itself. I understood in an instant that the pain people force on others was once forced on them. Some step off the pain path and find peace, while others do not.

I felt compassion for all of those who could not see what I could see: forgiveness is the only way to end suffering. Forgiveness is the only way to eradicate all the anger and hurt and the fear underneath it all from my heart.

Forgiveness is the only way they can never hurt me again. Forgiveness is the way to reclaim all of my heart for love. I picked up a ginkgo leaf and closed my eyes. Waving the tiny fan next to my cheek, I felt the slightest breeze drying my tears, and the world was sweet again as I realized forgiveness is the best revenge.

Grebe Coming and Grebe Going

17
Life's Kindling Point

One bolt of lightning can burn an entire forest down. Its destructive capacity can also paradoxically create new life. I felt as if I had been struck by lightning, causing life to reach its kindling point within me. Life igniting from the devastation was as intense as the painful way it happened. Both events changed me. In an instant I was transformed, immediately initiated into the world of violence. I understood I would be different now having no explanation of why or how it could happen. I only knew it was terribly wrong that it did.

Though I still looked like a child, I was no longer young. Experiencing the cruelty people are capable of altered me forever. The vulgar way it happened did not diminish the sacredness of life beginning within me and the strange duality of the pure and the profane. The wonder of conception was not weakened by the violent way it happened; they were always separate. The hurt, fear, and anger I felt about one did not taint the love and wonder about the other. Accepting the odd duality of life was something I had become accustomed to. People are capable of such valor and malice. I had already seen honor and horror. This was another level that terrified me. I had no explanation for how I was certain I was pregnant and sure it was a son. I did not think this was strange at the time.

I felt the unshakable devotion a mother feels for her child that in my inexperience and educational deprivation I had never imagined, wished for, agreed to, or saw coming. None of that mattered. The feeling of loving him came automatically. There was no hesitation in my heart, no debate in my mind, no vacillation in my spirit about doing what I had to do to keep him safe. It was clear what was best for this tiny being. Understanding now better than I ever had before the assault that I was not safe made it matter-of-fact for me to accept that the pain of separation had to be endured, for my child's well-being.

I knew he did not deserve the way he was conceived and that he did deserve to be raised by adults who were capable and ready to be parents. I had to give him the best chance to thrive and selflessly suffer the deep hurt of letting him go. I knew I had to find the strength for him. That is what good mothers do. My only uncertainty was how I was going to survive my grief of letting go.

I imagined perishing just after giving birth, and the thought gave me a sense of relief. I thought it would be a graceful way out of the enormous anguish after our separation. Part of me wanted to birth him healthy and strong and just let go of my own life.

I never spoke to my father about what his barroom friend did while he was passed out on the couch in the same room. I did not trust my father, but I did love him. My father had moved out after I suggested that perhaps he could be happy if he did. For a few years after, he would often come over when my mother was working late. Like the night the baby-faced monster came over and changed my life on a most profound level and moved out of the state that night.

I did not tell my mother because I thought the strain might finally break her. So I carried my secret like I carried the child, until my pregnancy started to show, and I had to tell my mother. Her response was as always, "Whatever you want to do, dear." She trusted the way I made decisions only when my heart and mind agreed. I had made up my mind minutes after the assault, and I did not ever change it. She respected and honored my choices and never lectured or doubted me.

When my father noticed I was pregnant in my eighth month, he pretended I'd had an affair and said, "I guess we should have gotten you some of those little white pills." I did not dignify his comment with an answer or even a glance.

Years later, the daughter of my father's second wife told me what she had not yet told anyone else in the family. During the time I was raped, my father had been raping her for several years, since she was seven. Her sharing this horror with me gave me the confidence to share my distrust of my father with her. I told her I had a haunting suspicion the baby-faced monster had received my father's permission to rape me. She told me then that she overheard a conversation between them in which my father said, "What Clare needs is a good fucking."

I understood that what I intuited years earlier that my father felt the need to break my spirit to control me was accurate. He feared anyone he could not control. He controlled my siblings through insults, threats, and violence. But because of my mother, and my desire to emulate her, he could not make me hate him or myself. That terrified him and was the reason he let his friend rape me. I believe they thought they would own me if I got pregnant.

They understood rape has the power to destroy a person's sense of self-worth. But it could not destroy mine, because I refused to let hate stay in my heart. My mother gave me the gift of understanding that my heart was meant to be full of love. So I found a way to forgive them both, and I found the strength to only love and protect the innocent being within me. I told him many times a day while carrying him, "I love you," and I have sent that message ever since.

Leaving the hospital without him was excruciating, but I had no doubt I was doing what was right. Giving him the best chance gave me incredible strength.

My father came to give me a ride home from the hospital without my knowledge or permission. I think he hoped I would be broken, and finally, he could control me. He studied me as we rode down the elevator with a couple and their new infant. I focused all my attention on the mother with her newborn infant across from me. We were eye level in the wheelchairs the hospital required us to leave in. She looked at me with such loving softness, and I felt she understood everything. Giving birth had opened her heart to understand without speaking a word. As we smiled at each other, my father almost lost his composure. For once, I knew what he was feeling. He was terrified. He stared at me probably thinking, how can she not be crushed? How can she smile at the woman leaving with her baby, while she is leaving without her own?

He had no way of understanding how I could be at peace. He couldn't understand the love involved in sacrificing for what is best for one's child. The way my father looked at me changed from that moment on. I do not know if it was out of respect or fear. Perhaps my father could only respect what he feared. Maybe it was his shame in setting me up to be raped. He could not imagine how I could be at peace. How could I not crumble? He could not fathom how someone who refused to hate could not be broken by someone else's hate. I followed love, while he ran away from it. Our paths did not cross or run parallel even while we were right next to each other. He was in anguish about his actions, I was at peace with mine. I had learned to be comfortable with the paradox of the fact that some go through similar experiences and end up hating, while some end up loving. I focused on my courage to do what was most loving for my son, not the brutal way that life reached its kindling point inside of me.

Electric Shore

18
Playing With Paradox

One of my parents was a creature of gigantic gentleness, like a blue whale, the other a creature of unpredictable ferocity, like a lion. The improbable combination of such different beings as my parents was only the first conundrum in my life. The spark of my particular life landed in the womb of an exceptionally kind person, but I was still not safe there. My mother's selfless consideration could not protect me from my father's selfish shame turned to violence. I always felt safe with one parent, and I could never let my guard down with the other. There was so much paradox in the life I was born into, so to be at peace with it, it had to become my playmate.

My father wanted to name me Roxanne, but uncharacteristically, my mother insisted that my name was Clare Eileen. When I asked her why she was certain of my name, she answered emphatically, without hesitation or explanation, "That was your name!" Clare means clear and bright, and Eileen means light. Roxanne means bright and radiant one. Both of my parents chose names that sound totally different but have the same meaning. How did they both choose a name that meant bright? My mother chose the name that also meant clear. How did she know that was my name? Did she know who I would be before I was born, or did her naming me create who I became? Am I trying to live up to her belief in me, or did her belief in me guide my journey here? Some of the most interesting questions may never have answers, but that does not mean we should not ask them and keep seeking answers. It does mean we should find a way not to be tormented by the conclusions we may never have. Living with paradox is part of life.

My mother's upbringing made her remarkably enlightened and humble. My mother was born in rural Massachusetts to a hard-working Irish Catholic mother and an abusive, alcoholic father. She was told her severe asthma was caused by inhaling baby powder as an infant that someone left near her crib. The doctors suggested she would do better in the city, so she was separated from her mother and siblings and sent to live with her unmarried aunt in Boston.

My mother's health often kept her from attending school. She loved learning and she read voraciously. Her aunt had to work most of the time to support them, so my mother had to often endure severe asthma attacks alone. I believe this had a powerful influence on her spiritual enlightenment. Perhaps the adversity allowed her to acquire an acceptance most never reach. She came to understand we are in control of only how we handle what happens to us, not what happens to us. She reached a light-hearted spiritual wisdom.

I never saw her lose her patience with anyone, except once when a boyfriend accused me of being promiscuous, and a different man once said my mother did not love me. Both times she showed that she did indeed feel righteous indignation when it was called for. Even then, she did not say anything unkind. She simply cleared up their confusion and her unequivocal support of my honor. My mother was always honest and open with me about her thoughts, feelings, and history.

On the other hand, my father never spoke of his family or upbringing. I knew very little about his childhood, except he lied about his age to join the navy when he was seventeen. He contracted tuberculosis in the Second World War and was sent back to his hometown, where he lost a lung. After he left the hospital and his hometown he went to San Diego to convalesce. He never mentioned that his mother came to help him recover. I found this out through my cousin sharing a newspaper article. My father did not return to his hometown until he went back with my brother, who wanted to see where he grew up. They arrived unannounced the day after Leon Sr. died, more than twenty years later. My father did not speak of his brothers, sister, or father. He only ever mentioned his mother.

My father was either feverishly pursuing a new endeavor, raging, or morose. He was always the center of attention whenever people were around. His quick wit, storytelling, and no allegiance to truth made him very entertaining. He was charismatic and needed to always control the conversation and circumstances by any means necessary. Certainly, he was very funny and interesting, but I was always waiting for the devastating insult about anyone who challenged or threatened him. I did not enjoy his gift of gab as strangers did.

He was compelled to dominate every gathering, not because he enjoyed doing so, but out of some dark need to control. I observed that fearful people need to control, while loving people want to support. My mother wanted everyone to be heard, and my father wanted everyone to hear him.

I developed a shield of silence so he could not figure out what mattered to me and demean it as he did to my siblings. My survival technique worked to spare me his cruel insults. So instead of demeaning me, he isolated me by saying I was his favorite. I did not blame them for resenting me for being spared his denigrations. This foiled his plan to get me to become hateful even after a pillow was held over my face, or a car cigarette lighter's red coils were pressed against my uncovered arm, or when I was hit in the back of the head with a solid glazed ball of rock hard clay, or my older sister woke me up in the middle of the night when she was on speed and pinned my shoulders to the bed holding a needle in her shaky hand to pierce my ears. I had the presence of mind to stay still so she would not pierce my cheek instead.

We all took on some of my father's anguish. I did not blame those who did not figure out how to stay out of the line of fire of his fury. Only my mother did not take on his pain. I chose to follow her path. I came to see the paradox that the one who appeared to be strong was really the weak one, and the one who appeared weak was really the strong one.

Pelican Sunset

19
The Clairvoyant Dance Contestant

The train clicked down the track with a constant rhythm for my first trip alone away from home. Before this, I was shackled by the judgments of those who knew or heard of my father or older sister. Their boisterous anger preceded me everywhere I went. I was his daughter or her sister, but now I was free of that association for the first time. No one knew them before they met me. My possibilities were as open as the landscape out the train windows.

Finally, now that I could be anyone I wanted to be, who did I want to be? Did I want to be a famous surgeon's daughter, or from royalty or diplomats, or the daughter of a well-known artist, or a Nobel Peace Prize recipient, or a chess champion, or a world-renowned violinist? Maybe I should be an orphan or a descendant of a silent picture star, or a president, or an Indian chief. Of all the lives I considered, the only one I was intrigued by for more than a moment was being an orphan in search of her true identity. But who I really wanted to be was simply me.

I could be me without anyone knowing any shocking details of my life, like how sheltered I was from other people or ordinary situations. No one would know that I had my first friends and conversations recently or that my father's barroom buddy raped me while my father was passed out in the same room. It would be my secret that I was afraid of everyone who was bigger than me—men because of their lust, women because of their jealousy. I was exhilarated by the idea that people would have no information, preconceived notions, or prejudices, that for the first time I would be seen for who I was.

The train made a stop at a tiny town in the middle of the night. A petite woman got on with a sleeping baby in her arms and two small children holding on to her skirt. She surveyed the car and came over to the seat next to me. I could see she was frightened and exhausted. In one look and a nod, we both understood she was escaping danger. As the train rolled down the track, we spoke of many things, but we never spoke of what or who she was getting away from. Just before dawn, she said, "Promise me you will never marry a man you cannot talk to!"

"Yes, I promise." These words gave her comfort and peace, and finally, she fell asleep and looked like an angel in the dawn light.

When we pulled into Albuquerque, she and her three children were all still sleeping. I wanted to stay and watch over them. A tear came to my eye knowing I could not. My struggle was my struggle, and her struggle was her struggle. I felt that our meeting helped us both, and that was enough. She was small but strong. I was young but brave. We would both be okay, but it was hard to leave her on the train. I said a prayer for their protection, and I got off the train.

My friend Janiece was waiting at the station and excited to see me. "What's wrong?" she said, seeing my sadness.

I did not want to speak of it, so I replied, "I'm just exhausted. I'll be okay."

Later that night, Janiece and I went to the movies. While in line, I asked Janiece, who loved talking about boys, "Of all the boys you know, who would you like to see again?" She described a boy she had not seen in two years. I wasn't really following her fast-talking and too many details. A few minutes later, she screamed as the boy she spoke about walked up.

Later that night, I heard her say to him, "My friend Clare knew you were coming. She has psychic powers."

The next night, we went to hear live music in a dance hall. On the way home she said, "What about the guitar player? He seemed to really like you. Do you like him?"

"He is nice," I said.

"But do you like him?"

"Not like that, and he has a girlfriend."

"Did he tell you?"

"No, but you can tell."

"You can tell because you are psychic."

"Anybody could tell, and I wish you would not say I am psychic anymore, especially in front of other people."

"Why? You should be proud of it."

The next night we went back to the dance hall, and the guitar player came over to me nervously and stumbled with his words not able to get them out. I said, "It's okay that you have a girlfriend. I just want to be friends."

"Who told you?" he shouted.

"Nobody told me."

"Then, how did you know?"

"You can just tell," I said.

"Oh yeah, the lead singer told you, didn't he? He is always trying to ruin things for me."

He was angry and threatening the lead singer, so I said, "Janiece, what did I tell you last night on the way home when the lead singer could not have told me anything."

"Clare said you had a girlfriend."

I said to the guitar player, "See, you know I did not talk to the singer last night, so he could not have told me."

Janiece said, "Clare knows things. She is psychic."

"Stop it," I said to Janiece, but it was too late.

The guitar player said, "Okay, if you're psychic, tell me about the other band members' love lives."

I thought I would say a bunch of incorrect specific stuff, and they would both leave me alone. So I said, "The lead singer is always talking about his conquests, but he's really never been with a girl. The piano player has been with the same girlfriend since junior high, and she just had surgery. He is very worried, but she is going to be fine." I was just about to speak about the drummer when I looked at the guitar player's face. He looked at me like he'd seen a ghost. Then I looked at Janiece, and she also looked frightened. Without wanting to, I was right about the two guys. I could see that Janiece thought I could see her secrets too, and she was afraid of me now. Janiece and I never spoke of it again nor did she speak freely with me again. I decided then and there not to ever do that again, as no good could come from it.

The next night at the dance hall, there was a dance contest with a cash price. I needed the money to get home. I did not tell anyone that I knew I would win. I laughed inside when the music started, and they chose "Black Magic Women" for the contest. I used the money to buy a train ticket home. I was relieved to be going home to my mother, who was not afraid of anything I could see. She always knew things that she could not explain. She trusted the mysterious information and only used it to help others. She was comfortable with the unknown origins of what seemed to be psychic to others but was normal to us. When I told her I knew I would win the dance contest, which I only entered to get the money to come home, she laughed and said, "That makes sense because you are the clairvoyant dance contestant."

Japanese Crane Mating Dance Posing, Trumpeting, Mating, Afterglow

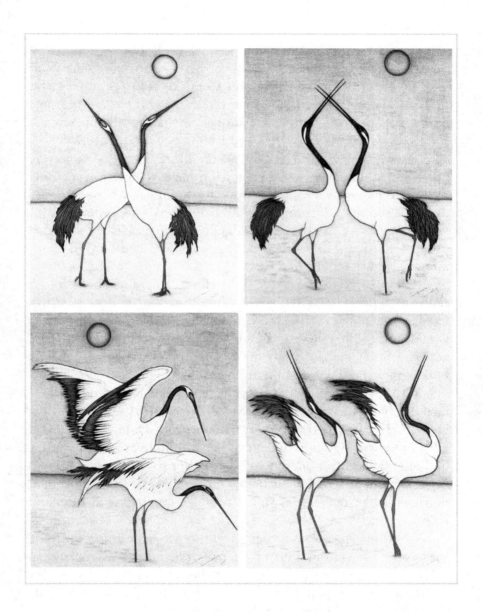

20
Sea Sick Soul Seeks Serenity

He looked like a painting of Jesus with his golden hair landing on his shoulders. His eyes were the color of the sea, his flesh tanned by the sun bouncing off the water. He ate no meat and wore nothing made from animals, including his shoes made from recycled tires.

My skin was olive. My nearly black hair had a copper sheen in the sun. My eyes turned from hazel to chestnut with my moods. I made everything I wore by hand with a needle and thread. I did not adorn myself with color, make-up, or jewelry.

We were both comfortable in silence. His eyes had a sadness in them ever since seeing war. My eyes stayed alert, knowing how people could be.

He worked every day on turning his fishing boat into a sailboat. The boat did not yet have a motor, compass, storm anchor, or radio. He planned to sail to Mexico. He assumed I would come but had not asked. Often no words were spoken, which was natural for both of us for different reasons. We had both survived dangers by remaining silent.

After he had a dispute with the harbormaster, despite the fact the boat was not seaworthy, he decided to sail to the next harbor. He calculated we could make it from Dana Point to San Clemente with the light and steady wind coming from the east. I had only sailed from one side of the harbor to the other. This was my first time at sea. I went below for a nap when the wind died down, and the ocean was still. I was not familiar with the calm before the storm.

When I woke up soaking wet, he was standing in front of me pushing a wetsuit into my hands. The boat was rocking so wildly I could barely get to my feet. Putting on the wetsuit over my damp body was difficult, but the thought of dying wet, half dressed below deck gave me the energy to pull it on and go up top. I was sure that if my life was going to end, I wanted to at least be up top feeling the wind and water.

As soon as I got to the deck, he demonstrated by straightening his legs against the side of the boat with his back against the tiller, the only way to keep the bow of the boat pointed into the waves. Without a word exchanged, I took on my duty. I understood if the boat turned and the wave hit us sideways, we would capsize and drown. It was obvious that death was a real possibility. I pushed with all of my strength against the side of the boat as wave after wave came. I wondered if my legs would give out before the storm did. How long could I keep it up? He tied a rope around the tiller and then around me so I could not be thrown overboard. He moved around the boat, bailing out water and tying things down.

The size of the waves was staggering. When we dipped into the trough between the waves, I waited anxiously for the next wall of water to rise above the mast. Each wave could be the one that was going to crush us, but each time the boat would rise, the powerful water would pass under us. I tried to use my arms to give my legs a break. Death seemed inevitable. Which way it would come seemed the only uncertainty. Would a wave crush my tiny body in a moment of unimaginable weight? Perhaps I would survive the impact of being tossed around at sea for a while before swallowing water instead of air. I fantasized about untying myself and trying to swim to shore. I thought at least I would die fighting instead of just waiting for death to come. My urge to jump overboard faded as I realized I could not even guess which direction land was, let alone hope to reach it. After I went through every possible way I could imagine dying, the only thing I was certain of was I wanted to survive.

I counted the seconds between my stomach spasms to give myself a focus other than death. For a while I wretched every fourteen seconds. Then a rage came up like a sea monster from my own depths. I felt anger at the harbormaster for throwing us out before we were seaworthy. Then I felt a rage at him for not telling me before we set sail there was a storm coming. Then the outrage turned toward myself for not asking any questions before putting my life in his hands. I noticed how fear and anger drained me. At eighteen, there was so much more I wanted to do. I decided staying tied to the tiller was the only chance of surviving. Thinking of death lost its interest, and I resolved to hold the boat steady for however long it took. I hoped that I could survive, and the resolve to do so gave me energy.

The only thing I could focus on now was what I would never know or understand if I died. Thoughts of the ineffable captured my undivided attention. I drifted in and out of thinking about what could not be explained. My thoughts that had first raced between fear and hope now moved slowly and powerfully, like the surges under the surface of the stormy sea. I noticed I was keeping the bow pointed into the waves without the tremendous effort it took hours ago. I stopped doubting my strength and ability to endure.

A calm came over me. I felt as if I was being watched. I considered my desperate situation might have influenced my ability to be rational. I could not reconcile this in my mind, but this did not concern me. I felt the presence strongly, and somehow I felt safe, and that was enough. Perhaps something mysterious was listening, and it was time to speak. I composed my words carefully. With great deliberation, I decided to take the opportunity to make important promises. I knew if I did survive, I would have to keep them. Being careful to promise only what I could honor, I promised to recommit to the choices I made as a child to be kind, honest, and awake. I promised to try not to take anyone for granted and to appreciate everyone and everything. Last, I promised to be brave and true to myself as the captain of my own life.

The waves were hypnotic. After I made each promise, I stared into the rising water thoughtlessly. My survival was clearly out of my hands, which was oddly comforting. Nothing bothered me anymore, not my stomach spasms, not even the idea of death. I had surrendered. He was scurrying around the boat bailing out water. He never stopped. I never moved.

I had no way of measuring time passing. Was it minutes, hours, or days? I said nothing. He said nothing. I noticed the waves decreasing in size and frequency. Neither of us celebrated. I realized I had not noticed him during the storm. This seemed strange since the boat was thirty-eight feet long.

When the seas settled down to nearly normal, he put up the sails, but the boat just turned in circles. The pressure of the waves had broken the cotter pin in the tiller, so it just spun in circles under the water. This made me laugh. He was not amused. He made smoke signals in a flat pan by burning paper in it to signal for help. We drifted for hours. I could see land in the distance. I had never found it so lovely before.

Finally, a small motorboat with two men came up beside us. They tied the boats together side by side and powered into the next harbor with the tiny flat-bottomed boat the only one steering. I heard them talking about how the waves break right at the entrance of the San Clemente harbor after storms. The men smoked a bowl of hashish. The smoke from their pipe blew across my face. I felt elated and did not know if it was the smoke or that I was alive. The men discussed one tiny miscalculation and both boats could crash against the jetty surrounding the harbor. This did not frighten me, and as we entered the harbor, I went to the front of the boat and held onto the jib line like I was riding a Brahma bull and gave out a loud uncharacteristic yell. When we were safe, I thanked him, our rescuers, the boat, the sea, and the mysterious forces for our safe return. I knew I had to keep my promises and say goodbye. My seasick soul had to search for serenity somewhere else.

Peace At Sea

21
The Rope Swing And The I Ching

After my mother's home in Southern California, I spent a brief time living on a boat with my first boyfriend. Then my first home was a tent on some undeveloped land in Northern California leased to Joan Baez for The Institute for the Study of Nonviolence. Many days were spent in blissful solitude, wandering in the woods, laying in the warm grass, and writing poetry.

My father lived in Palo Alto down the hill with his new wife and her eleven-year-old daughter. On one of his visits, he put up a rope swing in an oak tree close to my tent. I wondered if he was trying to be the father he had not been while I was a child. His motivations were rarely obvious and were most likely not as they appeared. I accepted I might not ever know his real reason for anything. I relied on my instincts for guidance and looked for subtle clues into his true intentions.

Sometimes my dreams gave me information that seemed to prepare me for things that had not yet happened. Other times, I got warnings around me that I could not explain but were clearly helpful. Then there were times I looked for answers in unlikely places. Like when my father went to Southern California and brought back the sailor boyfriend I had left.

Neither of them told me they were coming. I saw them sitting outside my tent drinking beer. I disappeared into the oak trees without them noticing me. I went to a friend's teepee to contemplate what to do. Why did he bring him without telling me?

The *I Ching: The Ancient Chinese Book of Changes* was there. Throwing the coins, I consulted the oracle for guidance. Being that I had an older and younger sister, I laughed out loud when the book said, "Father decides marriage for the middle daughter."

I went back to my tent and handed them the book open to my reading, saying, "I hope you two will be very happy together. I have plans of my own," and I walked away.

I did not see my sailor ex-boyfriend again until many years later. Out of compassion, I returned to the harbor where I got off his boat after the storm. I hoped enough time had passed so we could be friends. He was still angry and still drinking beer.

The choice to be the captain of my own life felt even more correct now than years earlier when I made it. Returning to my tent, I wondered how accurate messages can come from such sources as I sat on the rope swing reading the *I Ching*.

Stick Tossing Siberian Crane

22
Muffins And Magic

Marisha considered flirting an art form. She wanted to teach me the basics even though, as she put it, "You are not likely to ever get it." Taking it upon herself, Marisha decided to show me how to get guys even though I wasn't interested in learning to flirt, especially with the guys she selected. Looks appeared to be the only consideration she made, saying unapologetically, "I like cute guys." What they had to say did not matter to her. The first time we went out together, I made an attempt to converse with the men she selected for us to flirt with. I failed miserably. She said, "You intimidated them with real talk." The next time I tried to think of something unintimidating to say which ended up with me editing everything that came into my head. Then she said, "You scared them with silence." I tried superficial conversation, but she said it came off as patronizing. It became clear to us both I was not going to succeed at being convincingly superficial enough to flirt successfully. She concluded it was her duty alone to do the flirting, and I should not even try. I was relieved.

But not fitting into the prevailing customs made me think of my mother, who did not want me to be different than I was. So I called her, and during the conversation, she said, "I had a dream you got arrested."

She started to tell me the details of the dream, but I cut her off saying, "I'm fine, Mom. Don't worry."

Later that day, Marisha picked me up and we went to The Catalyst Cafe in Santa Cruz. She found some guy she thought was cute while I was writing in my journal. She came over to me, saying, "Now don't blow it this time. Come meet his friend." A sense of dread came over me, and I did not want to participate, but she had a kid going to the circus look in her eyes, and I did not want to disappoint her. As she went outside with her latest conquest from her guy safari, she signaled for me to follow. She got in the back seat of a car parked out front and gestured for me to get in the front. I did not want to get in, and as soon as I did, I felt it was the wrong place to be. I could not explain it. It just felt like a mistake. I looked at her giggling in the back seat, trying to get her attention, hoping she would see the discomfort in my eyes.

The driver was older and distant. When he started the car without saying a word, I said, "Where are we going?"

He answered, "Does it matter?"

"Yes!"

"Why?" he said without looking at me.

"It always matters to me where I am going!"

"Relax," he said. I thought, even if Marisha is so mad at me that she won't go out with me again, I do not care. I don't like this guy.

So I said, "Why don't you just take me back since it is clear we are not going to get along."

"Why are you so uptight?" He sped up and turned down a small street. Terror passed through me while my mind focused on reviewing my options. I had a terrible feeling about the situation. Systematically, I looked over my choices one by one. I could throw open my door and jump, but how could I get my friend out of the back seat when she doesn't even know we are in trouble? Maybe the guy in the back seat is okay. If I ran, maybe I could get help. By this time we were on a back road in the middle of dark redwoods.

Panic started, and I noticed I was holding my breath, so I forced myself to take a deep, slow breath and then another. Silently, I asked the universe for help as he pulled over. Immediately after my plea, I saw red lights flash on the ceiling of the car. I could not withhold my glee, and I whispered, "Thank you!"

The driver gave me an evil look as the police came to his window. The cop smelled the pot they had smoked earlier. He asked to see in the trunk. They found something they took to their squad car. I said to the driver, "You are going to tell them we just met, and we have nothing to do with whatever they found in your trunk." He turned his head slowly and looked at me with icy eyes. His mouth was twisted in a sneer. He made one snorting sound that never turned into a word.

We were all taken to jail. When I was given my one phone call, I called my mother, and as soon as I said hello, she said,

"Oh, you're in jail, dear." A few hours later, Marisha started to panic. For the first time in her life, she couldn't leave when she wanted to.

I was also feeling claustrophobic, so I stuck my fingertips through the open window through the small metal bars and started saying in a tiny voice, "I'm free, I'm free!" It made Marisha and the prostitute in our cell laugh, and we all calmed down.

When they brought us dinner, the prostitute noticed I did not eat and said, "You have got to eat."

I answered, "I don't eat anything I can't recognize."

She banged on the cell bars and yelled, "Bring this girl something to eat she can recognize." They brought me an apple, and I ate it.

The next morning before we were taken to court, Marisha and I were each given a one-size-fits-all tent dress. My dress was torn all the way down the left side. I held it together with my right hand because the officer who took us to court handcuffed my left hand to Marisha's right hand. Maybe she only had one pair of handcuffs, or she thought we would run. When my name was called in court, and I was told to approach the bench, nervously I stood up quickly and immediately pulled Marisha out of her seat. She tripped and fell, jerking me forward and forcing me to catch myself with my right hand, which had been holding my torn dress together. When it opened, I was exposed to the courtroom full of people. Everyone but Marisha and I laughed. Even the judge could not contain his smile at our slapstick first court appearance. By the time I got to the bench towing Marisha behind me, the entire room was in a better mood, except me. I was so embarrassed that I did not remember what the judge and my court-appointed attorney said before we were released without bail and ordered to return on the date set for our hearing. We were taken back to jail, given our clothes, and set free.

When we returned for our hearing, the driver still did not mention he had just met us and we had nothing to do with what was in his trunk. The guy in the back seat had been released on bail and did not show up for the hearing. We heard he fled the country.

We were ordered to return in two weeks for the next hearing. At the next hearing, the driver still did not tell them we did not know each other or have anything to do with the drugs in his trunk.

A friend of mine who worked at the cafe where we met the driver told me that the driver came in every morning at 11:00 a.m. and had a bran muffin and milk. My friend overheard him saying that I was a witch who had done a spell that brought the police. I called Marisha and said, "I will be picking you up tomorrow morning. We are going to talk to the driver while he is at the cafe."

She sounded terrified. "What are you going to do?"

"I'm just going to talk to him."

"What am I supposed to do?"

"Just sit down next to him, and do not take your eyes off him, and say absolutely nothing." So at 11:05 we looked through the back door and saw him sitting facing the windows.

I instructed the trembling Marisha, "Just sit in the empty chair on his right. Don't say a word even if he talks to you, and don't take your eyes off him. When I get up, you get up, and we leave."

"I don't know." She was so scared.

I got impatient with her and said, "You got us into this. Now I am going to get us out of it! It's no big deal. I'm just going to talk to him. Walk in, sit down, stare at him, get up when I do, and leave with me. Got it?"

Reluctantly, she said, "Okay."

"Good, now take some big breaths and follow me."

We walked up from behind him, and I took the chair opposite him at the same moment she sat down beside him. He was just about to bite into his bran muffin, which he put back on his plate. I looked at him for a few long silent seconds before I said with precise enunciation, "It is time to tell the truth." He started to get that twisted half grin, half scowl he had when I asked him to take us back to the cafe the night we met. It appeared as if he was preparing to say something but couldn't figure out what, so I repeated, "It is time to tell the truth."

"Why should I?" he asked with his sardonic grin beginning to surface.

I spoke clearly and a bit louder. "You know how bad your life got when we met? It could be worse." He crumbled his bran muffin in his hands. "All you have to do is tell the truth." I stood up calmly, pushed in my chair, and Marisha followed me out.

The next day our lawyer called and said, "All charges have been dropped against you both."

Nest In Lavender Wattled Crane

23
The Veils Reveal What Is Concealed

It is said that Halloween is when the veil between worlds is thinnest. That Halloween I dressed as a woman from India, veils concealing my body and face. A darkness I had not seen before was revealed.

There was a party in the house where I had a bedroom in the attic. My father had a room on the second floor. Everyone else in the house was close to my age, and they thought my father was cool and entertaining. He would have made a great charismatic cult leader if he could have managed his anger long enough to gain loyal followers. Many saw his ability to always be the center of attention as strength; I saw it as insecurity.

That Halloween, my father was dressed in only a white cloth folded like a diaper, and he drank his beer out of a baby bottle. Everyone was dancing, and my father came toward me dancing in a lewd manner. He had never done this before. I was disgusted and moved away from him quickly, leaving the room. Never wanting to see my father as perverse, I thought perhaps he did not recognize me under the veils I was wearing. I was so upset by his inappropriate display of sexual interest in me, his daughter, that I went upstairs to my attic bedroom.

When I got upstairs, two people were sitting on my bed talking. The woman I knew had a crush on me, and the man was a ballet artist who admired my free form dancing. The three of us talked, sitting up in my bed with our heads against the wall until very late in the night long after the music from downstairs stopped. After all was quiet, the three of us fell asleep on top of the covers with our costumes on.

I was awakened by stomping footsteps coming up the stairs. The steps were loud, deliberate, and exaggerated for dramatic impact. My first thought was my father was probably playing one of his twisted games to get attention. He then began reciting Shakespearian sounding morose prose. Just waking from a deep sleep, I do not remember the words. The tone was clearly meant to terrify, and the stomping was to portend doom.

As he got to the top of the stairs, I could barely see him in the dark. The moonlight lit his silhouette through the attic window behind him, so I could see he was carrying a shotgun. As the other two woke and sat up, I could feel my male friend shaking next to me as my father slowly lifted the gun and put the sight in front of his eye. Aiming it at my head, he said, "Sit together so it only takes one bullet."

I felt anger and took a deep breath. Strangely, I do not remember feeling fear. Perhaps growing up with danger close by I had learned not to let it overtake me when I needed to be clear. I channeled my outrage into a calm, clear voice, saying, "How could you point a gun at me? I have only treated you with kindness! What happened to you? How can you be so confused? I am not afraid of you. I feel pity for you!" Without another word, he put the gun down and acted like it was no big deal as he walked back down the stairs.

Not until twenty years later did I begin to understand what happened that Halloween night when the veils were thinnest between the worlds and revealed what had been concealed for years. For the first time, my sister told me that when my father pointed a 22 rifle at my head that night, she had told him earlier in the day, "If you touch me again, I will kill myself."

My father said, "Then I will kill Clare." She was fourteen, and my father had been sexually abusing her for seven years.

By her own admission, I had always watched over her. But still, she did not warn me back then. I forgave her and saw that she had lost the value of her own life by the assaults, so how could she value mine? The veils revealed what had been concealed—love and hate, life and death, good and bad can all get twisted together. May we all untangle the confusion and let our dark places get the illumination they need to be seen and healed. May all our concealing veils fall away. May we find the courage to see what needs to be revealed.

93

Migration Across Moon

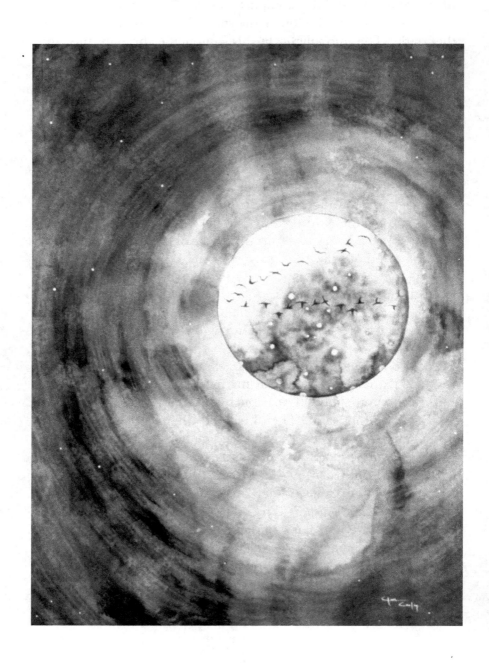

24
Deported Transported

On my way to a remote island off the west coast of British Columbia, I got deported from Canada, which oddly turned out to be the best thing that could have happened.

I would not have thought traveling with my father was a good idea if I knew that he had been molesting a child for years, or that he set me up to be raped by his barroom buddy, but I did not know these things until years later.

When I agreed to go to live on Valdes Island with him, the worst thing I thought might happen would be isolation. I have always loved being close to nature in serene environments and had an enormous ability to stay inspired creatively. Solitude is fine with me, in fact, usually preferred. So I imagined it would be a fine situation because I had no idea of the danger that he had hidden from everyone.

Looking back, it is a wonder I survived and can write this now. I have no religion because I see how it divides people instead of bringing them together. Most believe their beliefs are correct, and the other people's are not. I believe what spiritual beliefs have in common is what matters: and that is love, truth, and compassion. These are the principles I believe in. Maybe because I believe in these things, this is what is true in my life. Perhaps there is a benevolence in the universe that watches over me because I believe there is. Could this loving invisible force have orchestrated my deportation, transporting me away from danger? As with all the deepest questions, I may ponder, I may never have an answer.

Certainly, I have gone through some very painful stuff, but all of it has made me more understanding, tolerant, broad in my scope, so I do not regret any of it. Somehow, I have come through much without losing hope. Perhaps this is proof enough of an invisible innocence and ineffable love.

I am grateful that somehow I did not end up on a remote island with my pedophile father. Instead, the border guards searched his vehicle until they claimed they found a teaspoon of marijuana seeds. How did I know to immediately claim they were mine? Did I see it as an escape from the danger I had not yet consciously known was there? Do I have an invisible guardian watching over me, giving me a way out? Do I have common sense that told me to say they were mine in order to be taken away from the harm that certainly would have been in my future if I continued to be with my father? Most likely, I will never know how this event happened or why my instinctive, immediate choice was to say it was my trunk they were found in, but I do see how it saved me from peril, and I am grateful.

Because I said the seeds were in my trunk, they arrested me. I hated the feeling of being locked behind bars under someone else's control, but somehow I was confident that I would be fine. The sheriff's wife brought me a huge plate of fresh vegetables when she heard I was a vegetarian. I thanked her, even though I was not hungry. Later, when she came to pick up the tray and saw I could not eat any of it, she came back and pretended to be washing the walls just to keep me company. I was too upset to speak, but it was comforting that I could feel her concern.

A little later, I was brought before the judge in the same building. He never looked at me but kept his eyes on his desk, shuffling papers. I felt he did not want to be swayed by seeing my youthful innocence. I plead not guilty because I believed the guards put the seeds in my trunk to keep us out of Canada. I did not blame them for disapproving of my father; he made no attempt to be acceptable on any level ever. His long hair and full beard, hippy clothing in a truck with a homemade shell covered with paintings by my brother of plants that looked like they grew on another planet. Everything about my father and his truck stood out as anti-establishment. He telegraphed his disdain for anything conventional. I wore only my own handmade moccasins and baggy beige clothes. No jewelry or makeup with my hair long and straight, the way it grows naturally. I dressed that way in an attempt to call no attention to myself. My desire to be invisible only made me stand out. Most thought I must have been a member of a spiritual community no one had yet heard of.

Me claiming the seeds were mine threw their plans off, and no one knew what to do. Without my knowledge or approval, my father called my brother, who paid the three-hundred-dollar fine, and the Canadian guards took me to the border and said I would have to walk across the border to the American side. My father was not there to see me off. Nor did he give me any money. I had only the handmade clothes I was wearing and an over-the-shoulder bag containing my bamboo flute, journal, a pencil, a small knife, roasted soybeans, dried nuts and fruit, and twelve dollars cash.

When I got to the guard on the American side, he insisted on getting me a ride, and when a safe-appearing couple crossed, he asked them to drive me south. I was too traumatized to speak. They were sweet and stayed silent along with me.

I asked them to take me to a gas station at the edge of town. There I waited until a single mother came in for gas and asked her for a ride. I drew with her children and kept them happy while she drove. Mothers would always offer me food and shelter. In one woman's house, she left her kids with me while she went shopping. I would clean, cook, repair anything I could while watching over the kids. None of the kind people wanted me to leave, but I needed to get back to my mother. She was the only person I felt I could tell my truth to, and I needed to speak about what had happened to heal.

Only once in the almost 1,500-mile journey from Creston, Canada, to my mother's house in Southern California did I stand by the road hitchhiking. In Eureka, there were so many hitchhikers, I had no choice. So I made a cardboard sign with a drawing of the Golden Gate Bridge and stood at the end of the long line of hitchhikers with the huge sign in front of me so no one could see me. I politely turned down a number of rides. No women ever stopped. I accepted a ride from someone I thought was a gentleman. He was Dutch and called me his nature girl. He did a lot of talking, and I listened as he took me all the way to my mother's house. I arrived with the same twelve dollars I was deported with, and transported back into serenity.

Anhinga Kimono

25
Owl Eyes

When I returned to Duluth for a visit and decided to stay, I had trouble making friends, and I could not understand why, so I knocked on Kay's door to try and find out. In order not to lose the courage to speak my truth, I decided to blurt it out as soon as she opened the door. As soon as I saw her backlit in the doorway, I said, "Did I do something to offend you?" We were both stunned and silent until I continued. "If I have, it was unintentional, and I would like the opportunity to apologize for whatever I did to offend you women in town."

"No," she said, "you haven't done anything."

"Then why won't any of you talk to me?"

"Well," she hesitated for a while and continued, "Cause nobody trusts you."

"Why?"

"Cause you're pretty. Nobody takes you seriously."

"I thought that was what men did."

She laughed and continued, "We figure 'cause you're pretty, you are taken care of by a man."

"I have never been taken care of by a man. I don't have one single piece of jewelry, clothing, or any other kind of gift from a man."

"Yes, but you could."

"So, let me see if I understand this. Even though I don't have or let men take care of me, I could, so that is enough reason for you all to ostracize me? Well, that is certainly open-minded and bighearted. Maybe I was wrong about wanting to be friends with you guys. Perhaps you are not as interesting as I thought you were."

She got a kick out of my candor and started laughing, which got me laughing, relieving my nervousness. We laughed until our bellies ached. Then she looked at me with tears in her eyes from laughing so hard and said, "Fuck 'em. It ain't your fault you're pretty." We started laughing again as she pointed at my baggy handmade colorless clothing covering me from head to toe, saying, "You sure don't try. You look like a nun." She stopped laughing and her face turned sad. "It really isn't fair," she said apologetically.

"It's okay," I said.

"No it's not. And it isn't all of it. We don't trust you because you don't gossip."

I was shocked and said, "I'm the one you should trust because I won't be talking about you when you leave the room."

"Yes," she said.

Realizing what time it was, she said, "I have got to get to work."

As we descended her apartment stairs quickly, I said, "I figured out today what I am going to be for Halloween tomorrow. What are you going to be?"

"I'm going out as a bunch of grapes made out of purple balloons. And you?"

"I'm going to be a snowy owl." A moment later, we heard a resounding bang against the stairwell window. We looked at each other and ran down the rest of the stairs without a word. When we reached the alley, we saw a snowy owl standing perfectly still on a fence post about six feet away. I froze and she touched me softly on my shoulder without a sound and backed away leaving the owl and me. The owl was facing away from me, and without moving anything but its head, it turned completely around and looked straight at me.

Terror rushed through my body for a moment, and I held my breath. A voice in my head said, "There is nothing to fear," and I began to breathe again. The little white owl looked into my eyes, into me, through me. I felt its gaze like the wind passing through me as if I was no longer solid. We looked at each other without moving for what seemed like an hour. Time stood as still as the snowy owl and I did. My fear transformed into awe. I did not move until the brilliant white owl turned its head slowly forward and flew away.

Later in the night, Kay called me to ask, "What did your feathered friend say?"

I answered, "Everything . . . without a single word."

Then she asked what I was hoping she would. "Would you like to join me on Halloween? But you have to promise to slow up on the gossip a little," she said with her adorable giggle.

She picked me up with her purple balloons tied all over her body and matching purple tights and face paint and one huge green leaf on top of her head.

I was wearing a white, knobby sweater and knit hat that fit around my face and tied under my chin to cover my hair. I tucked little feathers around my face and put black lines around my eyes. I wore brown tights and brown gloves sticking out of the end of my feet with three fingers of the gloves stuffed with tissue paper to look like bird feet.

The bar she drove us to before the party was full of loud longshoremen dressed up like longshoremen. I sat facing forward at the bar hoping no one would notice me. I have never been comfortable in bars.

I heard some guys behind us talking about the bird at the bar. Then I heard a man come up from behind me and slap a quarter on the bar, saying, "Play the jukebox, girly." I stared straight ahead without moving. I did not want to dignify his disrespectful demeanor. He slapped a second quarter on the bar and said louder, "I said play the jukebox, girly." I turned my head, keeping my shoulders facing forward and my body totally still and looked through him the same way the little owl looked through me. He looked terrified and backed up until he hit the wall. He felt his way along it without taking his eyes off me until he felt the door. He fumbled around until he felt the doorknob, turned it, pushed it open, and ran out.

The bunch of grapes came over and said, "He was outta here like a stray dog when the dog catcher comes. What did you say?"

"Nothing."

Her purple balloons jiggled as she laughed, saying, "That snowy owl showed you how to look inside a guy, and he sure had something he did not want you to see."

Chrysanthemum Cranes

26
Stevedores On The Unsalted Sea

Behind the Longshoremen's Hall at five in the morning, the great lake was ominous when I got in the extras line. Lake Superior is to be respected in any season; the depth of its cold can take the warmth of life out of a person in minutes. The unsalted sea is so vast it creates its own weather and does not warm up below the surface.

Perhaps I would not have shown up if I knew what many said, I was the first woman among the longshoremen, the stevedores. But after my family came for a visit, and the court gave me the choice of my four-year-old nephew going into an overcrowded home or me taking responsibility for him, I became highly motivated to increase my income honorably.

Keeping my head down, the two guys in front of me did not stop talking or pay any attention to me. They did not notice I was a woman under the many layers of men's clothing and steel-toed heavy-duty boots with my hair tucked up under a Stetson hat.

By six o'clock, there were a hundred guys in the extras line. It was like a bar—everyone talking and nobody listening. Perhaps it was a strategy to keep warm, and it made it easy to disappear in the commotion.

Hearing the stevedores were beasts, and the work required a knife, I brought my best knife with a horn handle and a sharpening stone. Having something to do while waiting in the line on the bitterly cold morning seemed like a good idea. Knowing I would probably be the smallest person there, I thought having a good knife could make me look less vulnerable. The knife and I were very familiar, as I had cut a lot of leather for the handmade sheepskin coats and mittens I made.

I didn't show up to liberate women; I showed up because the money was better than anywhere else I was willing to work. I had recently been hired at the Black Bear Lounge during the day when the waitresses were wearing long dresses. But when I got home and opened the box containing my uniform for working nights, it had white lacy panties under a black skirt that did not cover my butt and black lacing across the low-cut top, so I quit before I started.

When I brought the uniform back, I told the women in the office I found it infantile and humiliating. They said, "Don't worry. You have a cute body." I realized they did not understand, so I left the box on the desk.

When my friend told me the shipyard was hiring women to load the boats, I thought it would be difficult but honorable work. He had not mentioned no women had shown up yet. When I got to the extras sign-up list, where non-union workers had to sign up, there were three names on it. Since I had listened to the two guys in front of me talk about broads, hockey, and politics for two hours, I knew their names. So I scratched out the name of the guy who had not been in line.

I couldn't imagine "Clare" being projected across the hall on the loudspeaker at callout, so remembering my father wanted to name me Roxanne, I spontaneously signed in as "Rocky."

When I came back at seven o'clock for the callout, the dispatcher assigned the union guys to their boats, then he read from the extras list top-down, adding however many guys the day needed. Over the loudspeaker, the names of the two guys in front of me were called, then "Rocky" followed by about ten other names. All of a sudden, this gigantic man pushed people out of the way to see the sign-up sheet and yelled, "Who crossed me out?"

He was well over two hundred pounds, and everyone around him stepped back. He looked around the hall, shaking and ready to punch somebody. I thought he was going to pick the smallest guy in his vicinity and break his jaw, so I walked up behind him just out of reach and said, "I crossed you out." He spun around and noticed at the same moment as everyone else that I was a woman. His mouth dropped open, and there was an audible gasp in the hall. I continued, "I got in line at five o'clock this morning, and there were only two guys in front of me, and you weren't one of them. So I thought it must have been a mistake. It is unfair to the rest of us in the freezing cold line waiting our turn for someone who is not there to be third in line.

So I crossed out the name of the guy who was not there, which apparently was you."

No one said anything. No one breathed. He wanted to punch me so bad he broke into a sweat even though the hall was freezing. You could almost smell his brain short circuiting as he tried desperately to figure out who to hit. A couple guys stepped up just in case he swung at me. Finally, the dispatcher said over the intercom, "We got things to do here!" And everyone started breathing again.

I tried to act like nothing out of the ordinary had taken place even though I was terrified. Not having anticipated this reaction, I tried to play it off like no big deal, like I hung out in the Longshoremen's Hall with the guys all the time, crossing bullies' names off the extras list.

Everyone was relieved when he stomped out of the hall yelling. The dispatcher finished reading off the list saying, "Okay, you guys . . . and lady, you know where you're supposed to go, so get going! You don't get paid for standing here."

Most of the men stared as I walked by, but the more composed of the group at least closed their mouths. By the time I got to the boat, everybody knew a woman was coming. Even the foreign sailors were gathered around the railing, staring unabashedly down into the hold.

My first day was the hardest all season, which I think was the intention of the higher-ups wanting to discourage females. So I was sent out on the twine bale boat. Two twenty-pound twine bales were tied together in an awkward forty-pound shape that was impossible to carry comfortably. To lift them onto the top row of the pallet I had to boost them with my thigh. I was solid black and blue from hip to knee the next day. Carrying the forty pounds of twine in one hand threw my spine out of alignment, even when I switched back and forth, so I tried carrying one in each hand and moving slower, which felt better. The guys saw me struggle with the top row and offered to help me. I replied to every offer of any assistance, "Thank you very much for the offer, but if I can't do the work, I shouldn't be here, so no thanks."

Being the first woman felt like a responsibility heavier and harder than the twine bales. There was always someone watching me.

105

By the first break on my first day, most of the guys had bet on whether my knife or the union guy's knife was sharper. One of the guys must have seen me sharpening mine in the extras line. He said to the guy who was always bragging his knife was the sharpest, "I'll bet the lady's knife is sharper than yours."

I didn't hear his response, but I am assuming it was something like, "No broad has a knife sharper than mine!"

"Want to bet?" About thirty guys came over with the oldest longshoreman who they appointed as the judge. They asked for my knife and held up both knives for everyone to see. Mine had a brilliant sheen and was perfectly clean, which they expected, but the size of my knife surprised them. First, the old man cut a piece of paper with the longshoreman's knife. Then he sliced through the paper like butter with mine. A gasp was heard, as there was no question my knife was sharper.

The men started exchanging money with the guy who lost. Shocked by the outcome, he said, "I don't believe it! That's not her knife."

To which I replied, "It's my knife, and I've made a lot of sheepskin coats and mittens with it."

"I believe it," the guy who started the bet said, grinning. I contained any show of delight on my face by pressing my thumb on my sore thigh until my urge to smile passed, constantly feeling aware I was setting a precedent for any women who followed.

At lunch, I declined their invitation to go to the bar and have burgers and beers. All I wanted was to get off my feet for as long as possible. It was also very clear to me I wanted no opportunity for anyone to think I was flirting with anyone. Eating the healthy food I brought while I sat with my feet up was refreshing. Even walking up to the deck to see the water was more effort than I wanted to put out. I rested every chance I got. I was determined to keep up knowing the slower crew got no break between loading each pallet. I did not want to be the reason my team got no breaks. I ate and leaned my back against the wall with my hat covering my eyes. After lunch, I noticed it was easier to keep up. Most of the guys had slowed down considerably, digesting greasy food and alcohol.

During the afternoon break, a couple of guys pushed an old man toward me, saying, "Come on, sing it!"

The old man was embarrassed that they were pushing him, so he said sternly, "Okay, okay."

"Hello," I said, watching his cheeks turn crimson, contrasting his white hair and gentle blue eyes.

One of the guys shoving him said, "He wrote you a song."

He looked down and began to sing, "They called her Roxanne. They thought she couldn't do it, but they found out she can. She looks like a woman but works like a man." It went on rhyming innocently as his voice cracked and trembled.

"Thank you," I said and bowed toward him, which made him grin. The guys all laughed.

By the end of the day, I was the only one maintaining any kind of pace. Most of the guys started drinking beer at lunch and then switched to the hard stuff. They did not eat well or lacked sleep, and many had hangovers. I ate a healthy breakfast, lunch, dinner, and fig bars with fruit juice at every break while I rested with my feet up.

One of the guys said, "Slow down, you're making us look bad." Without any alcohol in my veins, I noticed the deep cold lake and the ten-degree air. It was painful to stay still. Moving was my only way not to freeze.

After dinner, before any of the crew got back to work, a rotund union guy came over to me and said, "I'm bumping you." By the look of bewilderment on my face, he realized I had no idea what he was talking about and continued. "I'm taking your place. Go home." He had a very disrespectful manner, so I wanted to resist doing what he asked, but I was exhausted and glad to be done. There was no way I was going to quit before the job was done, and this gave me a way out.

I gathered my stuff and was climbing the stairs out of the hold when a couple of the guys I had worked with all day said, "Where are you going?"

"A union guy bumped me."

"No way. He's not going to stay home drinking beer and watching TV and then bump you just to get your overtime pay!"

I protested. "It's okay, really guys. Let's not start something my first day out."

They were all talking. No one heard me. One said, "I'm going to tell the other guys," and bolted.

Within minutes, everyone on the boat was gathered up on the deck and yelling. I was frightened. I thought, great, the first day a woman works on the boats and there is trouble. A few guys came and escorted me to the deck, saying, "Sit here and don't move." I was scared by the bully in the hall, but this was truly terrifying.

I was imagining a union guy throwing me overboard, remembering being told the Mafia ran the Longshoremen Union. Then I saw a serious-looking guy walking up the plank onto the boat, yelling, "What the hell is going on here?"

A guy who worked across the hold from me stepped up and said, "She worked hard all day, while some union guy sat on his butt and he thought he was gonna come here and take her overtime pay. No way."

There was shouting back and forth until somebody shouted, "If she goes, we all sit down, and you don't get this boat out of here."

The crowd behind him yelled, "Right!"

The boss yelled, "Okay, shut up, you guys." He looked through the crowd and said, "How could such a little thing get anything done? You guys want her around 'cause she's something to look at!" My heart hesitated to beat while waiting for some response.

"Actually," one of the biggest guys said, "she gets work done. She carried two of the twine bales at once all day long. She's about the only one still getting anything done around here. Let's get back to work and see if we can keep up with her!"

There was more discussion at a lower volume before the big boss turned and walked down the plank. We all went back to work until ten-thirty when the ship was fully unloaded.

At home, I soaked in hot water, still feeling the ship swaying beneath me. Even though all my muscles hurt, I laughed thinking about how the guys who had been described as animals stood up for me. Animals respect each other, I thought. People can be the confusing ones like the bullies, but the fair people outnumber them.

Many people treat others well. We should walk away from those who do not. They stood up for what was right for a stranger. I was delighted it was such a positive experience. I was proud of the stevedores—the day I became a stevedoress on the unsalted sea.

Snow Dance Japanese Cranes

27
Aurora Borealis And Working Girls

The only way for me to get the 1,284 miles from Libby Montana to Minneapolis, Minnesota, in time for Kay's baby's birth was to hitch rides on long-haul semi-trucks. So I stood at the top of a long slow-climbing hill where the vehicles were going slow enough for me to see who was in them. Most I let pass without putting my thumb out.

The policies I learned hitchhiking have proven helpful in all areas of life. Do not get in if the driver is in a hurry or gets annoyed while you ask as many questions as you need to feel comfortable. Safe people understand you need to determine whether or not they are safe. Bad people often try to rush things. Always stand where others can see you. Wait until someone is passing and wave-like you know them before getting in the vehicle, letting the driver see there is a witness. Do not make critical decisions when tired, upset, or hungry. Remember, bad actors can have a good act. Like everybody, but don't forget that trust needs to be earned. Stay alert and be kind and cautious. Keep in mind you are the one keeping yourself safe.

After being assaulted in my mother's home with my father passed out on the couch, I was afraid of everyone larger than me, which is almost everyone but children. Most sexual assaults happen by people we thought we could trust. I accepted that I could triple lock my doors, have a number of different alarm systems, weapons, a mastiff, German shepherd, Doberman pinscher, and a pit bull, and still, I would not feel safe. Only if I learned to protect myself could I ever become comfortable in the world with other people in it. I was inclined to mistrust my own potentially dangerous species, and for good reason. I could stay inside a fortress and give up my freedom, or I could set out to face my enormous fear. I set out to regain my sense of being safe in the world by being aware and logical. Ironically, the only assaults I have endured happened at home with people who had the trust of not only me but other intelligent, mature people.

Never once out in the world among strangers did anyone attack me. I was actually safer among strangers I chose to be with than those that had access to me in my family home or once when a roommate slipped drugs into my tea. The assaults happened when I let my guard down in my own home, as I do not do out in the world.

Pete pulled his cab-over semi-truck off the road, and I went to the driver's side to talk to him where I was visible to the road. He did not get nervous as I asked him lots of questions. I followed all my policies and then walked over to the passenger side to get in. He liked to talk without any concern about what. He was a decent and simple man, which was just what I hoped for. Smart men, when they are not good, can be very dangerous. I set out to get to know him by asking lots of questions about his family, wife, and kids, and where he was from. Did he like trucking? What would he rather do? What are his favorite activities? Where did he live, and how much time did he spend driving? He did not tire of talking, and I did not tire of listening. It was easy to keep him talking. I was genuinely interested in what his life was like, and I knew I may never spend this much time with someone like him again. I am curious about everyone, and it is easy for me to be friendly toward anyone respectful but impossible for me to fake it when people are rude. Another of my policies is just get away from disrespectful people as fast as possible. Pete was sweet.

When we stopped, he got an enormous amount of greasy food, and I got a baked potato with sour cream. Bill, a good looking man in a usual sort of way and aware of it, came to sit at our table. Pete was ample and round everywhere and a cute sort of homely. Bill suggested I ride with him, assuming I would prefer to ride with a handsome man. I politely declined, saying Pete and I were enjoying becoming friends. To break the tension my rejection caused, Pete asked Bill how his weekend went.

Bill said, "It was fine. I got drunk, went fishing, and got divorced."

I said, "How long have you been married?"

"Seven years."

"How long have you been thinking about getting a divorce?

"Seven years."

"Well, I guess then it is good you did it."

Later down the road, Pete told me the only females that ever come here besides the waitresses are working girls riding between truck stops. I did not get it and asked, "Working on what?" Pete got very uncomfortable, and I realized he was talking about prostitution. We both stopped talking for a while, and I tried not to show my shock.

After I composed myself, I said, "If adults want to do that, that is fine for them, but it would not be fine for me. It would make me very sad. I am not a working girl. I am just trying to get to my friend before she has her baby, and hitchhiking is the only way to get there in time. I hope you did not give me a ride because you thought I was a prostitute. I hope you are not disappointed."

"You certainly don't dress or talk like a working girl. You are different from any female I've ever met."

"What is the difference?"

"You are nice but not in a silly way. You are honest."

We both needed some quiet time and did not say anything for the first time since he picked me up. A little while later, Pete pulled into a truck stop saying he needed to sleep for an hour. He said I could lie next to him and rest too. I said, "I am fine right here, but go ahead and get some sleep." He asked if he could give me one little kiss.

"No," I said firmly. Then he asked if he could feel my leg just a bit. He tried a few more suggestions but did not touch me, so I was not afraid. I just felt sorry for him.

Then he said, "A guy has got to try."

"But a guy doesn't have to keep trying what he knows won't work." Just then, out the window were incredibly beautiful waves of green lights in the sky. The aurora borealis was much more beautiful than I had ever imagined it could be from the photographs I had seen. I was stunned by the crackling electricity undulating in strange, lovely patterns above us. Pete seemed unimpressed, which did not seem possible. I could not understand his lack of interest in the incredible show, and I decided to let him sleep and enjoy them in solitude. The dancing luminosity was memorizing, and I felt privileged to witness it. I was grateful Pete was quiet, and I could enjoy it without his need and loneliness talking and distracting me.

Several hours later, when he awoke, the lights had disappeared, and the sky was dark again. I felt sad and changed by all of it—the natural beauty, the human yearning, my vulnerability. I did not want to speak. He was clearly embarrassed and started driving without a word. He appeared ashamed of himself, but I did not think there was anything I could say to make it better, so I said nothing.

A few hours down the road, out of nowhere, Pete spoke about his wife not wanting to be intimate with him. He told me they got married six years ago because she got pregnant. "Now, five kids later, she has no interest in me. We get along better now that I am trucking, and when I come home, the kids are glad to see me."

I tried to help by asking questions like," Do you ever bring her little sweet, thoughtful gifts from the road? What does she like? Maybe she feels taken for granted and overworked. She does not get away from being on duty with five kids and staying home. Maybe she is just tired and feels like when you are home, she can finally just rest."

He started to tear up and was embarrassed, so I looked out the window but continued listening. He poured out all his troubles, most of which I let flow past me out the window, feeling like a sacred witness to his pain. I hoped my empathy was reaching him and helping him in some small way.

He asked, "You are a kind person. Do you believe in God?"

"I don't know. No one can know, but I do believe in kindness."

"How did you get the way you are so young?"

"My mother is the kindest person I know, and I guess I want to be like her."

"You are doing a good job. And you are right not to be a working girl. They don't really like men. They do it just to get paid. They lose sweetness."

"That is sad. I feel for them not figuring out a way to get by that doesn't discourage them. Doing the only thing most men will pay for but do not respect them for doing it. That is an awful life! I try to learn as many skills as I can, so I do not ever have to do something I would not respect myself for."

It was the end of the line for his delivery. Even though we knew we would never see each other again, we parted as real friends. I was better for getting to know the hardships of a decent man's life. We were both grateful I was not a working girl, and what I will most remember is the aurora borealis.

Heavenly Bodies

28
Heavy Happiness

When I was five, I asked my mother, "Why is my big sister mean to me?"

She answered, "She is jealous, dear."

"What is jealous?"

"Jealous is when someone thinks you have something they do not."

"I only have seashells, stones, and feathers. She doesn't like them. I don't have anything she likes."

"Yes, you do, dear."

"What?"

"Happiness."

"Why doesn't she have happiness?"

"Because she doesn't like herself."

"Maybe she would like herself if she was nice."

I thought maybe my sister would be nice to me if I wasn't happy. My brother wasn't happy, and she was not nice to him, so I decided to stay away from her but keep my happiness.

From then on, I hid from her meanness while searching for my own happiness. By her teens, her unhappiness was doing every drug she could find. By eighteen, she got pregnant with the boyfriend she was doing heroin with. Right after their baby was born, they were so far into drug oblivion they weren't feeding their infant. Realizing he could die without them noticing, I took him to Northern California while they were too drugged to notice. She did not try to find us and soon after left the area, so I brought him back to my mother's house where he would be well taken care of.

I told my mother we needed to be strong when my sister returned and not let her live in our mother's house unless she agreed to go into a rehabilitation program. I promised if my mother did this, I would figure out a way to get her in. My mother agreed, and my sister said she would go in but never went to sign up, saying the line was too long. So every morning at dawn I got in line to hold her a place in the methadone maintenance program. When they were going to call her name the next day she had no excuse left. I drove her and dropped her off. She got clean and came out of the program with a job as a drug counselor.

While she was in the program, I went to visit friends in Duluth. Many asked me to stay and teach creativity. It had not been my plan to stay, but using creativity to help others gave me great happiness.

I began teaching a class in adult education called A Way to Learn to Dance for Joy. Then I was hired to work in drug and alcohol rehabilitation centers, crisis shelters, and at a psychiatric hospital. Then I worked as an artist in residence for the public schools and the university where I taught my curriculum Dancing Into the Arts.

I created a peaceful and purposeful life for myself. Then my older sister showed up with her new boyfriend, I let them stay with me. A few weeks later I found out he had just gotten out of prison for manslaughter, and they were not interested in doing anything but drugs. I told them they needed to find their own place, and they moved to town into a house full of drug dealers.

Soon after, my mother, brother, younger sister, and my older sister's four-year-old son came for a visit. My older sister was using drugs, so I told her the family would visit her in town.

She got angry and went to the police and told them we had kidnapped her son. The police looked into it and knew about the drug dealing house where she was living. They knew about me because of all the work I did in town. They came to me and said, "You can take guardianship of your nephew, or he will be put in an overcrowded group home." My brother and younger sister went back to California, and my mother stayed until her asthma got so bad she had to leave.

So even though I moved two thousand miles away from my family, I still ended up caring for my four-year-old nephew alone. The difficult part was having to go to court and defend him against my now hostile drug addict sister and her dangerous friends. It took seven months of custody proceedings to decide where my nephew would be placed. At one of the appearances, my sister's friend came into the courthouse restroom after me and said, "If you were my sister I would kill you!"

I said, "I sure am glad we are not related."

The judge decided I should take my nephew back to live with his grandmother in California, which I did. But just weeks after I returned him to his grandmother, my older sister showed up and took him to Canada to live with our alcoholic father.

My nephew tells stories about living on the west coast of Canada with his mother and grandfather and having to fend for himself to eat. He would go to the local cafe and sit next to a truck driver and stare at his food until he would buy him something to eat.

Later, when my older sister got pregnant with her second son, she called our mom and said her boyfriend was abusing her. My mother drove up to Canada to get her and her son. She brought them back to San Francisco, where my mother had been living with me.

When her boyfriend showed up to meet his son, my sister would not let him in, and it became clear that my sister had been abusing him. He returned to Canada broken-hearted. My mother and his son's brother, who was ten years older, took care of the newborn for four years until the night my fourteen-year-old nephew showed up at my door at midnight. He said his mother and her boyfriend would hit him. They would go out drinking and leave a little food in the refrigerator and threaten to beat him if he ate it. I told him he could live with me. When she insisted he come back, he filed a petition with Children's Protective Services against her claiming abuse and neglect. She pled guilty to the charges, and the court placed him in my home again after ten years.

My mother, younger sister, and I had a meeting and decided the fourteen-year-old would live with me because I was a single artist, the four-year-old would live with my younger sister because she was married with two incomes and no kids, and my mother would get to not have to take care of the boys anymore. It was all going according to plan, and the four-year-old was happy with his new home and bedroom. It seemed like the dysfunctional family was finally going to function. But the plan fell apart, and all three of them ended up with me.

Then my older sister's attorney said just because she pled guilty to neglect and abuse of her fourteen-year-old, she was not found guilty of any neglect or abuse of the four-year-old. So the court returned the most vulnerable one to his mother without his brother or grandmother there to watch over him. My younger sister could not bear the strain of it all and stopped communicating with anyone in the family. I left her a message. "This is when the little one needs us the most," but my little sister never answered or returned the call or returned to the family.

The four-year-old was on his own with his drug addict mother and her dubious friends. I would call the authorities regularly trying to get someone to check on him. They would knock on her door, but she never answered. His preschool would call me regularly saying no one picked him up. I would rush over and keep him with me for as long as possible without upsetting my older sister, knowing if she felt threatened she would take him to our father in Canada, as she did with her older son.

Until one day she called me saying she did not have any asthma medicine for him. I said I would bring some to the hotel where she was staying with her girlfriend. When I got there, she barely opened the door and wanted me to just hand her the medicine. I got her to let me in, saying I had to see him to know which medicine he needed. He was having such trouble breathing I knew he needed to go to the emergency room. Her girlfriend was hiding from me in the bathroom, and when she went in to talk to her, I picked up my tiny nephew and ran to my car. I drove to the closest emergency room.

The doctor yelled at me, saying I should not have waited so long to bring him in. He could have died. I asked the doctor to put it in writing and took it to the Children's Protective Services. Finally, they had proof they could take to a judge, who then placed my four year old nephew with me.

She said she wanted her sons back but did nothing to make that happen. She did not even have to be sober. The court would have returned her children if only she had gone to an AA meeting once a week.

Years later, before the final hearing determining the permanent placement of her second son, she followed me into the courthouse bathroom. I wanted to have some kind words, so I started. "In respect to our deceased mother—"

Cutting me off, she yelled, "You have no right to speak of our mother. You wore white at her funeral."

The first thing I said at our mother's service was, "I am wearing white because my mother asked us to rejoice, not mourn, her passing because she is free and at peace now." I understood it was pointless to repeat this in the courthouse bathroom. She stomped out while I asked the universe to help her. I returned to my chair outside the court, and she went outside to have a cigarette.

Her lawyer came down the hall and said, "I see you are a kind person who is trying very hard to make peace with your sister, but you cannot because she thrives on conflict."

It was true, even though we both had a mother who was compassionate and celebrated the accomplishments of all of her children. We both had a dangerous father who competed with everyone. Perhaps being firstborn, she received the most potent dose of his rage. Maybe her heaviness was that simple. Perhaps my happiness was as simple as I focused on our mother.

The court gave me guardianship of her two sons, and we went home. Periodically, she would call and say things like, "You brainwashed my sons and turned them against me."

I said, "I know you know that is not true. I just want everyone to be happy. I love you! May I take you to lunch?"

She would hang up, but I was okay because I meant it. I do just want everyone to be happy.

Freedom Flight

29
Different Colored Folks In The Same Cosmos

"Pull over," I yelled when I saw the For Rent sign.

Sandy replied, "Not in this neighborhood!"

"Stop, please. I'll go in alone, and you can keep looking at the apartments on your list."

Sandy dropped me off, and I rang the doorbell.

An elderly woman's voice came through the intercom, "Mr. Greenfield will be right out to see you."

When Mr. Greenfield saw me through the glass door, his eyes widened, making them look enormous in his thin face. Opening the door without saying a word, he led me down the mustard yellow hall to their apartment, which was full of porcelain animals and dolls in bright synthetic dresses. It smelled of bacon.

Mrs. Greenfield called out, "Bring her in here." Mr. Greenfield pointed to the bedroom. I thanked him and went in. Mrs. Greenfield was tiny in her huge forest green bed. She was clearly in charge, and after she looked me up and down, she nodded to Mr. Greenfield, indicating it was alright to show me the apartment. He took me up to the top floor. The apartment was in the back of the building away from the street noise. The two bedrooms had a view of a wild hillside covered with purple nightshade and golden poppies. The hardwood floors had just been redone, and the walls were newly painted. It was immaculate, and I immediately felt at home.

We went back to Mrs. Greenfield, and she invited me to sit on her bed. We talked and laughed for over an hour about her peculiar poodle and how I made my own clothes and about the foods we liked to eat. Finally, when I told her I wanted the apartment, she looked at me seriously and said, "I hope you don't mind. We are all colored folks here. You would be the first white person to live in this building. But I like you, and if it's okay with you, it's okay with me."

I answered, "I'm colored folk, too, just a different color."

Laughing, she said, "I like you a lot." Then she yelled into the next room where Mr. Greenfield was pretending not to be listening, "I told you white folks could be nice."

For the next six months while walking home from my waitressing job, I passed the neighborhood barbershop. There were always at least five old men sitting there smoking and talking. One day the silver-haired man who was always in a three-piece suit stood up and yelled to me as I passed by the open door. "Can I walk with you?"

"It would be my pleasure," I answered.

"I don't want anything. I just want to walk with you."

"I can tell a gentleman when I see one. And I'd be honored if you walked with me."

"We've been watching you since you moved into this neighborhood. We decided you are okay on a count of you don't give anybody any shit, and you don't take any shit."

"Thank you," I said and bowed as we parted at my door.

I must have had a big grin on my face because as I walked in, the two women who were always at the front door like gentle sentries said more than hello for the first time. The curvaceous one in a very feminine dress said, "Young lady, could I ask you something?"

"Certainly." I answered.

"We've been wondering what you do. My husband thinks you're a playgirl on account of you are pretty and dressed up most times. But I said to him, 'No, she does something.'" She narrowed her eyes, looking deep into me and said, "I know you do something."

I said, "Do you want to see what I do?"

"Yes!" She answered with childlike enthusiasm.

"I'll be right back!"

I went to my apartment and picked up a sheet of slides of my recent watercolor paintings of the cosmos. I brought a magnifying glass so she could see them clearly. She studied the twenty slides for a long time without an utterance. When she got to the end, she started over and looked at each painting with the same attention as the first time. Then she looked a third time going back to the one of an avocado seed budding in turquoise space, then to the one of a sheep skull in maroon space, then to

123

the orchid branch in cool blue space, then to the waterfall in royal purple space, then the wave crashing on a shore of stars. Finally, after looking at kayakers paddling toward mountains made of stars, she handed the slides to her fellow silent sentry and put her head down and softly turned it back and forth. Then making a sound like a rodeo cowgirl doing a bird call, she looked at me with a huge smile and said, "You always look up, and when you do, you see everything!"

It was the highest sort of compliment to be recognized for who I am. We are all different colored folks floating in the same cosmos.

Flamingo In Deep Blue Water

30
The Articulate Bag Lady And
The Elegant Primitive

It never stopped making her laugh when I called my mother the "articulate bag lady," which came from her extensive classical education combined with her humility and lack of vanity. I loved that she named me the "elegant primitive," describing my self-taught aesthetic style.

I was a typical lost teenager in an atypical life when at fourteen years old, I proclaimed, "I want to be perfect."

In her gentle voice, my mother responded, "That's nice, dear," and looking deeply into my eyes, she continued, "as long as you enjoy the journey, since no one ever gets there." She had a way of speaking the harsh truth in a reassuring manner. "Accept your imperfections as perfect, dear." My mother's words were reassuring and motivating.

I did not know what to do with my life, so I asked the wisest person I knew, "Where do I fit into this world?"

My mother answered with calm confidence, "You are a visionary, dear."

My youthful lack of understanding snapped back sarcastically, "Oh great. That will look fabulous on a resume. They will be lining up to hire me!"

"You will find your way. You always do."

"I know what a baker and a cobbler do, but what does a visionary do?"

"Well, dear, some people see things as they were, some as they are, but some like you see how they could be." Though I felt no clearer about my direction in life, I felt better about my confusion.

My insecurity about where I belong in this complex world has gone through many transformations.

No longer do I wonder who I am or why. I am an artist, who observes and portrays observations. However, where I fit in may always remain elusive because of the lack of value placed on artists, visionaries, and freethinkers.

The world needs all different sorts to contribute to be whole. The more diversity there is, the healthier any environment and the world will be. The cobblers, painters, nurses, dancers, bakers, spiritual teachers, librarians, artists, plumbers, and visionaries are equally necessary.

My mother's education was impeccable, she graduated from the Massachusetts School of Art, the first institution in the United States to give a fine art degree. She was also visionary and spent most of her youth in books, accumulating tremendous knowledge, perspective, and humility.

Though we shared a fascination with creativity. I loved solitude, being in nature, and doing artistic projects. I was as academically uneducated as my mother was educated. Those were my happiest childhood memories, along with spending time in silence with her.

At thirteen, I feared that my father's ever-increasing rages were going to seriously hurt someone soon. So I mustered up the courage to say, "Dad, you are not happy. Perhaps you could be happy if you lived somewhere else." After he left, my mother got a job in a factory working a punch press. Before they married, my father told my mother he was sterile. She was pleased with this because she did not believe she had the physical strength to be a mother. She was raised Catholic, and birth control was not allowed. Four kids later, her hope of doing her art was replaced by responsibility. The only art she did was doodles on scraps of paper.

My mother had let go of religion long ago but was the most truly spiritual person I've ever met, free of resentment, selfishness, or regret.

She had exquisite bones and a radiant grace, with no vanity. She wore used functional clothing, and the most she would do for special occasions was put on red lipstick. When I was young, I would just stare at her, thinking how could she be so unimpressed with her own beauty. She was as humble as she was magnificent. I still marvel at how she could be so exquisite and unaffected by it. She was so articulate but never showed off her intelligence. She listened to me as if what I said had value even when I was unsure of myself. And when I only wore baggy, colorless clothing and no adornment, she said, "When you hide your beauty, dear, it is the rest of us that miss out, because we are the ones who see you." She let me come into my own in my own way, never pushing, but always gently encouraging. Any confidence I have comes from her always treating me with respect.

I was not ready to talk to people or have any friends until I was fourteen. Then in my twenties, I began to share my joy for creativity through dancing, painting, writing, and playing my bamboo flute. I taught everywhere I was invited until the bureaucracies started draining my spirit, and I feared I would lose the joy of creating if I stayed. So I went into my studio and drew every day for five years. Sometimes my lack of any training would frustrate me, and I would ask my mother for help. She would always say, "You follow your instincts, dear. That is your way and it works."

Sometimes I would be satisfied with this, but that day I kept pushing her, saying, "You've learned so much technique. Maybe if you shared it with me, I could figure it out faster."

"Be patient, dear. You always figure it out, and you quit when it is done. I worked with a lot of artists in school and the studio after I graduated, and I never saw anyone like you. You follow your inner guidance, and then you stop. Many artists quit or ruin their work by overworking it."

Still, I was not satisfied with her answer, so I got more insistent, saying, "I am stuck with this, and I can't figure out what is wrong with it. What is wrong with it technically?"

She took a deep breath and answered softly, "Well, dear, technically everything is wrong with it. The source of light, the perspective, the anatomy is all technically wrong, but none of that matters for you. You have your own way. You are the elegant primitive, and that is right. If I told you the techniques, you would just have to forget them to follow your heart. That is where your art and excellence comes from. You are so lucky. Just be grateful and trust yourself."

I did not doubt my process after that. I so appreciate my good fortune to have had the articulate bag lady as my mother and guide. I wish everyone to have someone to tell them the truth we all need to hear.

Hummingbird In Cherry Blossom Branch

31
The Sword Of Truth Cuts Through Confusion

As I called my stepsister, I knew she had to come see me, but I had no idea why. Neither of us questioned it when I said, "You have to come see me now! Leave your son with his father and go to the train station. I will not get off the phone until you promise you will!"

Hours later, she was at my front door. I opened the door and said, "Come in and sit down." I spoke as I paced the room. "I just met a woman, and within minutes we were sharing our experiences of having been raped. It amazes me how we can be such a powerful healing force in each other's lives by simply telling the truth."

As I sat down, my stepsister said, "I have something to tell you." The seriousness of her tone was unmistakable. "Your father started raping me when I was six, right after he married my mother. You are the only person I have told except my first boyfriend."

I had to focus on my breathing for a while before I could speak. I wanted to take a vow of silence for the rest of my life because there are no words that can change the past. There is nothing anyone can say to fix something like that. It felt arrogant to speak at all, but I knew I had to gather the strength to say something for her. I took a deep breath and said, "I believe you. As horrified as I am, and though I never imagined he could do anything like this, I believe you. I have always known he was broken. And as much as I never wanted to hear anything like this, thank you for telling me. I apologize you had to endure such terrible stuff like that."

Such a sadness came over me, and I had trouble taking deep breaths. The information that my father could be so cruel was devastating. I felt drained. Though I did not trust him, I had no conscious idea he could be so twisted. I felt my will to live evaporating.

Hours later, I told my friend I just heard the worst news I've ever gotten. After I told him the details, he said, "I am glad that's all it is." I told him I was confused by what he said. "It happened long ago."

"But for me, it has just happened."

Later in the night, I was too hurt to cry and too stunned to speak. I could not feel anything at all. It was as if my systems were shutting down—my life force was leaking out. I couldn't think of anything happy or remember anything joyous. I went to bed and stared at the ceiling for what felt like hours.

I fell asleep and woke up from a dream so real and terrifying it felt like I was dying. Too weak to stand up, I felt if I did not force myself to move, I could just stop breathing altogether. Pulling myself out of bed took every ounce of my strength and will. I crawled on my hands and knees to the shower, where I strained to reach up and turn on the water. I sat on the tile floor with the cold water hitting me, but I could barely feel it as the temperature went from cold to hot. As I recalled my dream, I felt my fear levels increase. I didn't want to think about it, but I could not shut it out. It became clear I had to face it. I said out loud to myself, "You can understand it. It is your dream."

Recalling it from the beginning in detail gave me something to focus on. The dream began with me descending concrete stairs into an underground space. There were three young women in silver dresses at the bottom of the many levels of stairs. They were dangling their bare feet in an underground pool of water, unaware of the danger that only I could feel approaching. Then I saw an older man coming down the stairs. As he passed an ax on the wall, he took it down. Everything in this subterranean world was gray or silver except the red handle of the ax. He picked up his pace as he continued down the stairs. I knew he meant to chop up the girls in the silver dresses, and I saw their red blood running into the water in my mind. I knew I had to get them out of there silently, without letting them know the danger was near. If they panicked, they would give our whereabouts away. Two older women in the next concrete room had no awareness of the doom approaching. It was up to me to lead them all out of this lightless underground gray world. As I gathered them all together, I signaled by tiptoeing and putting my finger over my lips to not make a sound. As the man came down the stairs, I showed them where to hide behind a corner as he passed by descending the stairs. The three young women and the two older women all followed me up until we were out of the subterranean world. I recognized we were safe on a lawn at San Francisco State University. Immediately, I understood the three young women were my sisters, the two older women were my mother and stepmother, and the man with the ax was my father. I felt strength coming back into my body.

In the next breath, I understood for me to recover I had to face my father. I needed to hear how he could do such a thing. A few months later, he came to San Francisco, and I told him I wanted to see him without mentioning why.

Without considering taking a weapon, I went to see him knowing I was going to be honest. Somehow I had no fear, and within minutes I said, "I know what you did. I need to allow you to explain why."

My father put his head down and began speaking. "I know what I did was wrong, and I would never do it again. But my wife was not interested in intimacy, and her daughter was affectionate, so I fell in love with her."

I was not expecting his response and I was stunned for a while before I could speak. "Even if you have talked yourself into believing it was love, just so you and I are clear, there is no way it was anything but a horrific assault of a child. It was abusive and damaging to do what you did to a six-year-old girl."

He did not defend himself. He did not say anything at all. He just stared at the floor until I said, "I am not your judge or therapist. I am your daughter, and I love you no matter what. However, to be in my life, you are going to have to make amends for what you did, and I cannot tell you how."

We were both silent for minutes until I said, "You are my father, and I know so little about you. What happened to you? What wounded or confused you to do that to a child? You cannot shock me now. I have already had to hear some of the hardest things a daughter can hear. You have this opportunity to be real and unburden yourself. Tell me what happened to you."

He said nothing, but the look on his face of shame and sadness was screaming, but no words came out. I thought perhaps he had covered his secrets with so much shame he could not uncover them anymore. Maybe he understands whatever happened to him cannot justify what he did.

I felt enormous compassion for him and I wanted to help him without minimizing his wrongdoing. Hoping to help him articulate something that might begin some healing, I asked, "You were in the war, but you have never spoken of it. What was it like?"

He answered, "Everything was profane."

Deep silence overtook him again, so I asked another question. "What are you afraid of?"

"Going to prison and being called 'short eyes.'" I realized his constant fear of being discovered and incarcerated and then brutalized or murdered by the other inmates was a terrible punishment he brought on himself.

"It is my stepsister you hurt, and I will support whatever she wants to do. She has no interest in going to the police this many years later, so I will honor her wishes. What I needed to do was face you. But if you ever do such things to another child, I will know, and I will stop you."

He nodded and offered to pay for my stepsister's therapy, and we parted.

She did not accept his offer, but I had an opportunity to introduce her and pay for her to join an incest support group. I had been asked to be a guest therapist. As I listened to the women speak, most of them mentioned wanting to scream about something going on currently in their lives. So when it was my time to make a healing suggestion, I said, "Let's all one by one scream into a pillow." I screamed in it, and then I passed it. It was one of the most powerful experiences of my life witnessing these victims of horrific abuse face their mortal terror of letting the scream out.

I did not understand until after the session that victimizers often say, "If you scream or tell anyone, I will kill you." Letting out the scream trapped within them for years had a profound healing effect on all of us. One woman dropped out of the group instead of screaming.

My stepsister joined the group, which meant I could not be a guest therapist anymore. So I found the funds and told her to continue until she was done without concern about the cost. She insisted on paying me back in cash. I refused and told her adding up the cost would interfere with her healing. She suggested that in exchange, she would make me a set of dishes I could design. I was delighted by this suggestion. We made the crane dishes she threw with her mastery according to my design requests. I carved a different crane species into each dinner plate and all the dishes with wetlands crane habitat motifs. I glazed them with a light green celadon, and she fired them in her studio. They were a manifestation of pain transformed in the fires of creativity into beauty.

One of the times we were working late into the night in the ceramic studio, she told me when I called her and insisted she come see me, she had her biggest kitchen knife propped in a drawer like a sword to impale herself as the phone rang. The sword of truth wedged in the kitchen drawer needed to cut through the secret holding her heart hostage. Perhaps I will never have an explanation for how I knew to call and insist she come see me. I do not need to know how or why. I just feel grateful I knew to reach out, and she found the strength to respond.

Facing Into The Wind

32
Ugly Art In The Beautiful World

The artists I admire do art for love, even those fortunate enough to sell it for money. One does not necessarily lead to the other. People said my work moved them, and some bought it. I want to create for the rest of my life. It is what nourishes my spirit, so I decided to see if it could be a viable business.

An owner of big galleries in San Francisco and one in Manhattan agreed to review my work. Though our meeting was at nine in the morning, he answered the door in his bathrobe. Before I entered, I waved to my male friend in his car, waiting for me to enter before he drove away. I made certain the gallery owner saw him and understood he was also seen. As I entered, I asked to use his phone and gave his address to the person who would be picking me up and told my friend I would call when the meeting was over, knowing the gallery owner heard me.

I knew it was going to be strange, but I did not feel in danger. I thought he will not be a gallery for me, but I'm going to learn something about how the art dealing world works. He offered me coffee with hard liquor that he was drinking, which I declined.

At first, he barely looked at my portfolio as he talked only about himself for hours. Every time he got a phone call, he told them to put off his next meeting, saying he was looking at some work. Then he started calling it some good work, which changed to great work. By midday, he said to cancel his appointments for the rest of the day because he was looking at incredible work, and he got increasingly flirtatious. He told me I was so formal and distant. To which I replied, "This is a business meeting." Then he said he felt like the frog, and I was the princess, and if I kissed him, he would turn into a prince. I told him I did not believe in fairy tales, even when I was a child.

Out of nowhere, he said, "You do not have to have sex with me to get into my gallery. You just have to act like you would at openings."

I responded, "No, I do not have to do that to get into a gallery because my work is good. Even if it wasn't good, I still would not do that," and I left.

I decided to go to New York and seek out a more professional response to my work. The absurd meeting made me think about how artists can easily be taken advantage of because many are sensitive, timid, or under-supported, making them more vulnerable. Predatory people can be attracted to artists for these reasons.

I was left with fifty dollars after buying my round-trip flight to Manhattan. I stayed for five weeks by walking everywhere I went and sleeping on a photographer friend's couch. I left every morning at dawn when she converted her living room into her studio. I would walk from gallery to gallery, then to the Metropolitan Museum of Art that was on a donation basis. I would end up talking with an older woman admiring the art every day without thinking about it. I have always enjoyed the wisdom and perspective of older people. Most days, they would invite me to lunch and never let me pay when I offered. I did just fine on one meal a day. And after walking to a few more galleries, I would return to the museum to rest someplace safe, like the Japanese Garden, until it was time to go back to my friend's in the evening to sleep. I did not need to spend my limited resources with this routine.

One day, while I was weeping silently in front of a Van Gogh painting, a man came over and sat at the other end of the bench. He was also crying without any sound. We talked a little, and I discovered he was an Egyptologist and restored paintings for the museum. He told me later over tea that no female museum visitor had ever spoken with him in the many years he had worked at the museum. It saddened me to realize people were so full of fear that they could not even talk to each other. He was married, and I was in a relationship in California. We parted knowing we would never see each other again, but we both felt better about people, and that was wonderful and complete.

I walked all over New York City, leaving my portfolio with gallery assistants in the hopes it would make its way to an agent or a gallery director. Attempting to meet with them directly seemed wrong. I wanted my art to stand on its own rather than being tied to an impression I gave off. Most gallery owners and dealers were men, and I was a young woman. In my five weeks in Manhattan, I went to over one hundred galleries and discovered only four were showing nature. Two were paintings done by old masters, one had massive art, and the last gallery was showing natural scenes in a twisted way.

Not one gallery was showing the kind of work I did, which can be described as dreamlike realism, or as my educated mother described it, elegant primitivism. To get an understanding of how my work would be received, I decided to show my work to gallery owners I knew would not be interested in my type of work, so they would have no reason not to be candid. One gallery owner said, "I am sorry to tell you, but your work is beautiful."

"Why would you apologize for saying my work is beautiful?"

"Because as you can see, I deal in ugly art."

I replied, "Yes, you and most of the other galleries in town. I approached you for feedback because your gallery has well done ugly art."

"Thank you. I can't advise you how, but I know you will do well somehow."

One afternoon, while I was sitting in a beautiful hotel lobby writing in my journal, a man asked if he could sit by me. We talked and he said he knew an art agent and offered to introduce me. I asked him to drop my portfolio with the agent. When I went to pick up my work in the Helmsley Building, I learned she had represented Andrew Wyeth. She said she had not seen a portfolio as deep as mine in a long time, and she would represent me if I moved to New York. I did not think I could stay healthy in the dense city without enough nature to refill my well of inspiration. Central Park was lovely but not enough and could be dangerous.

Instead of being discouraged by the lack of possible outlets for my work, I left Manhattan with increased motivation to continue what I was moved to do. The lack of representation of natural beauty in the self-impressed art world empowered me to be a visual voice for nature. People can be so full of their own importance. Many of us lack the humility to acknowledge before we existed and after we have perished that nature will survive. What's more, even if we bring our death upon ourselves—war, the decimation of natural places, pollution, or disease—nature will endure. We need nature; nature does not need us. I couldn't move to Manhattan because I accepted I needed natural beauty to thrive.

In New York, most of the galleries were full of art tantrums on canvas. It was the moment in art to forsake craftsmanship, grace, and loveliness—as if art had become a contest judging who could throw the biggest fit and get paid the most for it.

It all left me even more inspired to share my admiration for the simple elegance of nature. The urbanization of the world was leading to an abandonment of what was naturally beautiful, following instead the fashion of ugly art. If I was going to follow anything, it would be the laws of nature, not fashion.

I returned to my placid country home on Napa Valley's Silverado Trail, knowing I could not stay if I wanted artistic exposure. New York could not work, but San Francisco felt like a compromise. I could have exposure while maintaining the balance I needed. I decided to find a woman to show my work to. When I met with Edith Caldwell, she said my work was lovely, and she named many well-respected locations where it should be.

I asked her, "Why shouldn't my art be in your gallery?"

"Because I cannot sell peaceful nature."

I was shocked. "But you are the only one who tries."

She looked down as she said, "So I should know. People in the city don't buy serene nature."

"Why?"

"I don't know." She appeared perplexed.

"I have a theory."

Looking up, she said, "What is your theory?"

"People do not want to be reminded of what they have forsaken."

She thought about it and said, "As good a theory as I have ever heard."

I left feeling sad about what was reflected in the ugly urban art world. I also left more committed to sharing my art with a world in desperate need of reminders of nature. My art is a meditation on natural beauty. I do it because I need to, and people need nature to be restored. We do not need more reminders of human hubris. We need to come back into harmony by balancing artificial ugliness with natural beauty.

New York

33
Memoirs Of A Squid

Squids restaurant was a trendy hotspot where every type of creature in the sea of humanity swam. It was across the street from a Church of Scientology, up the street from the bus depot, and nearby a homeless shelter, it was never totally calm sailing.

Having recently moved back to San Francisco, and being newly financially responsible for my nephews and mother without any help from my siblings, I needed more income. I ran into the bartender from Squids, and he mentioned they were hiring. So I went right down and introduced myself to the woman behind the bar. Though she told me they didn't need the help, I slid my business card across the counter and said, "Give me a call if that changes. I have done everything from waiting tables and mopping floors to running my own restaurant in Napa Valley."

As I turned to walk away, she said, "Wait here." When she returned, she signaled for me to follow her to a table where another woman was sitting. The two of them asked a few questions before they asked if I could start the next day as the manager hostess. I told them yes, but I had a few requirements: my nightly pay needed to be separate from the tip pool, and I would not stay past closing. I would always show up sober, on time, not take bribes for seating people out of order, and I would watch over the restaurant and everyone in it. They agreed to my terms and handed me a set of keys to the office.

When I arrived the next evening, the staff knew nothing about me except I had the only keys to the office, which was alarming to me and resented by the crew, but I needed the job. The owners left town, giving me no instructions or introductions. All of this immediately revealed to me that this was going to be interesting and challenging. But, it was a job I did not have to think about while I wasn't there, allowing me to focus on my art.

Within minutes of arriving my first night, a small, homeless alcoholic stumbled in and tried to get the wallet out of a man's pocket. The man, who was seated with two women and was clearly trying to show off, jumped out of his chair and positioned himself to hit the old drunk. I got there just in time to get between them and say to the homeless guy, "Can we go outside and talk about this, please?"

He smiled and said, "Sure," while following me out the door.

When I saw the young man coming toward us, I said quickly to the homeless drunk, "Actually, I don't have anything to say." Leaving him outside, I closed the door behind me and stood in front of it on the inside to create a barrier between them. I locked the door behind me while the patron was threatening to kill the little old man.

I got in front of him and said firmly, "He will not be coming back in, and you are not going out there. What he did was not right, but he is living in the street with nothing to eat. Obviously, his mental faculties are diminished, which is why he would try such a desperate attempt at picking your pocket while you are seated."

"I should kill him and teach him a lesson," he shouted.

I said in a scolding tone, "His miserable existence is his lesson. Please go eat your meal with your friends, knowing he has no meal or friends." He threatened again to kill him. I said, "If you are trying to impress your women friends with your courage to take on such a formidable adversary, a tiny old man who cannot stand or think straight, you should know most women are more impressed by compassion than brutality." He went back to his table and sat down mumbling.

I brought the old man a small to-go cup of soup, and said, "Just ask if you're hungry next time."

He said, "Thank you, kind person," as he wandered away.

It became my immediate policy to watch the sidewalk and try to intercept desperate people before they wandered in and offer to bring them a cup of soup if they waited outside. For the pennies this cost the restaurant and how effective it was in keeping peace inside, it seemed obvious, yet the crew who had been there for years were astounded. I was amazed no one thought of it sooner when there had been brawls regularly inside.

My job was like a traffic cop at the intersection between heaven and hell. The most powerful tool I had was a kindness to redirect the dangerous ones back out of the door gracefully. I said the same thing to everyone no matter how they dressed or what they drove up in or whether they stumbled or strutted in. Everyone was greeted with, "May I help you?"

The homeless who wandered in while I was seating someone else would often say, "I am hungry."

I would reply, "I apologize, but I cannot give you a table. If you would be so kind to wait here," as I escorted them out. "I will bring you something to eat." Some would wander off before I could bring them something. This always worked to keep the peace. But if I was in the restroom when someone wandered in, it was chaos.

The crew thought I had some magical power. They said, "He has never come in here without a fight before. How do you do it?" I would tell them all you have to do is treat everyone with respect and show no fear.

The restaurant was where tourists would come to see the latest street fashions and cool people. I felt like a babysitter in punk paradise. Every night there were opera and theatergoers sitting next to pimps and drug dealers. The out-of-town people had no idea of the sort of folks they were next to. The bodybuilder busboy watched the door whenever I asked him to as soon as he saw the effectiveness of my ways and would tell me when dubious people came in.

One evening, I went into the empty auxiliary dining room for a moment to get away from the deafening music everybody else seemed to enjoy. I was standing by the huge plate glass window at the far end of the unlit room. Staring out the window taking a few deep breaths, I felt something ominous approaching. I turned around quickly to see a huge woman coming toward me really fast. Her shoe polish black hair was teased and piled on top of her head, making her nearly seven feet tall. She looked ready for a fight and like the sort of person who had been in a lot of them. The restaurant was so loud outside this room she could have shot me, and no one would have heard it. She outweighed me by more than a hundred pounds, and I had not ever been in a fight. She said, "I don't like the way you've been sticking your ass in my boyfriend's face."

Without hesitation I said, "Thank you for telling me." This confused and disarmed her just long enough for me to get past her and run out the door where the busboy who had been looking for me stepped in front of her. She stomped back to her table. The busboy had appointed himself my bodyguard, which I'd never appreciated more. He didn't take his eyes off her until she left. After she had gone, the crew asked me what happened, and we all got a good laugh trying to imagine me flirting with her emaciated greasy speed freak boyfriend.

Another night, a white man stuck his face into the phone booth where a black man was on the phone. The two of them were about to punch each other when I got there and said, "People are having dinner here. Take it outside if you need to beat your chests like a couple of gorillas." Getting them to focus on me instead of each other, I continued, "Come on, let's go out front because I want to see which one of you is the silverback." The white man left the restaurant. The black man finished his meal and then thanked me for stopping the fight.

One early evening, I saw three rough-looking teenage boys walk up to the plate glass window carrying two by fours. I did not have a good feeling about their intentions, so I went outside and said, "Hey, how are you guys doing?" They were clearly surprised I spoke to them.

The leader said, "Just out for a walk."

I pointed at the huge boards in their hands and said, "Oh, I suppose those are your walking sticks."

"That's right," the leader said and pressed his body up against me, pushing me into the window. He was trying to intimidate me.

So I asked, "What's your name?"

When he answered, I replied, "That's the name of my nephew I am raising."

Impressed that I was not scared or disrespectful, he said, "Hey, you have friends in the hood now. Let us know if you ever need anything, and we'll take care of it."

"Thanks. I appreciate it, but what I want is for you guys to take care of yourselves. And I think you should lose those walking sticks because they look like trouble. I have to get back to work now. Have a good night, and please be careful."

Then there was the night I was looking across the street and saw three men talking, pointing at Squids. Then two walked over while the third stayed behind. As soon as the two were outside the restaurant, they both started running toward the door. The first one started screaming, "He's gonna kill me!" The second man ran in after him, and the third one waited outside. While the first two were yelling and running around, the third came in looking for purses left unattended by the people who got up to see what was going on. I recognized the first man from a previous experience when he was intruding on two women who asked me for help. I asked him politely to give them space. He was the only person in the year I worked there who threatened me, saying, "Come near me, and I'll hit you!"

I said, "I asked you respectfully, and you threatened me, so you have to leave!"

Now months later, he was back with a plan to rob distracted diners. Luckily, the police had seen the robbery setup as they were driving by. They only caught one out of the three men, but they could not arrest him since he hadn't been successful in stealing anything. I asked if I could talk to him and said, "If you are hungry, you could have asked for something to eat. I have not turned anyone away. But now you are not allowed to come in here again. In fact, if you need to walk down this street, you'd better walk on the other side."

After he had gone, I offered the cops some food and sat down with them because it was the first time the police had ever shown up when called by Squids. It had the reputation of being so rough they didn't bother with it. I told the cops the people who work there told me they thought I was an undercover cop for a long time. The police said, "We know why, the way you talked to that thug."

"I don't usually talk like that, but he threatened me before, and tonight he was trying to rob us."

I always wore the same black pants and jacket that looked like leather but was Naugahyde to keep the smell of fried calamari from permeating my skin. The cook told me I looked like one of Charlie's Angels.

Everyone else at Squids had been there from the beginning. I was the only newcomer and the only one with the office keys. The owners must have hired me to scare the crew because someone was dealing drugs, though the owners did not tell me any of their concerns. I did not blame the crew for not embracing me under the circumstances. Raising my nephews and caring for my sweet sickly mother made the income crucial, so I did not allow it to bother me either. Being avoided by the rest of the staff during my shift made my job easier since I needed to stay alert to not miss danger approaching, and it was always close by. What mattered to me was that everyone stayed safe on my watch, not whether or not I was popular.

After I had been there for almost a year, I booked the extra dining room for my birthday and invited the whole crew and my friends. The attire suggestion was elegantly ridiculous, which was outrageously fun. Much to my delight and surprise, one waiter did a fire-eating act, another wore an enormous "Divine" mask, and a third did a hilarious skit of a baby with a huge head. We had a hula hoop contest and a photo booth to document all the creative fun. Perhaps inviting the crew melted their cool hearts. Finally, everyone was warm and accepted me. This made it bittersweet soon after when I got my sign that it was time to go. When I came to work one afternoon to find a familiar homeless man had been murdered out front, I gave my notice and took only the memoirs of a Squid with me.

Reverse Space Birds

34
Orchids, Apathy, And Understanding

As my mother passed by my floral arrangement, she curled two long, dangling blades of grass back up through the orchid stems, transforming their awkward shape into an elegant form. She was an aesthetic alchemist with a gift for turning the ordinary into the extraordinary. She had an eye for detail while being able to keep the whole picture in mind. Pointing out things to look at but not telling me what to see was her clever way of guiding me to expand my perceptive abilities.

While her lack of vanity allowed her to not notice or be concerned about her own appearance, from across the room she would call me over to remove an inch-long beige thread from my beige skirt. She would insist on hemming my dress to correct the slightest asymmetry, while her own used store clothing was usually mismatched.

I finally overcame any embarrassment over my mother's humble appearance at one of my exhibitions when I gave her a gorgeous flowing royal blue and silver dress to wear. Wanting to keep it perfect before the opening, she put a stained blouse over the dress to protect it while she ate. While I was talking to Josephine Landor, the artist wife of the founder of a globally successful corporate design company, I waved my mother over to meet my new friend. As we spoke, my eyes dropped to the dirty blouse she had forgotten to take off. When Josephine looked away, my mother said, "Oh I am so sorry, dear. I'll go take it off now."

"No, you are beautiful just the way you are. Don't go anywhere." Finally, I could see how exquisite my mother was, beyond my own vanity and her complete lack of it. From that moment on, her disregard for the superficial served as a test of the depth of others. I weeded out those who were bothered by my mother's appearance. Those like Josephine, who remember her as elegant, turned out to be the dearest of friends. My mother was many wonderful things, including a sincerity meter. Those who saw the qualities of her heart beyond her lack of attention to her exterior turned out to be internally exquisite themselves. Whenever a friend did not ever ask her to join us, I knew they were not deep enough to be lasting friends.

Once, just as I was arriving late to meet my mother for lunch on Haight Street in San Francisco, she was being escorted out of the cafe by two men, one under each arm. They were about to set her on the sidewalk as I ran up, yelling, "That's my mother. What are you doing?" They froze as I approached, and I took her to the closest chair. She pointed to her throat because she was choking and could not speak. I gave her a napkin and stood covering her from the onlookers saying, "It's okay, I'm here." She looked up at me, relaxed a little bit, and spit up a small chicken bone she had accidentally swallowed in their soup. We both started to breathe again. I hugged her for a long time. I felt a terrible rage.

She saw the fury in my eyes and said, "Clare, it's okay."

With the tears I was trying to hold back bursting out, I said, "What if I hadn't come when I did? They were putting you on the sidewalk." They had assumed because of her humble appearance she was a street person. They must have thought she was drunk because she could not speak while she was choking.

She said, "They see so much pain that they are numb. Not everyone has the strength to keep feeling and seeing without looking away like you, dear." She always called me dear, and she always meant it.

I said, "I'll get you some water." I went to the counter where the owner and the two men stood perfectly still. As I walked to the counter, everyone watched in silence. I picked up a glass, filled it with water slowly, and set the pitcher down. Everyone in the cafe held their breath, wondering what I would do or say. I brought my mother the water. As she drank it, the only sound in the cafe was her swallowing. When she finished it, we got up and left. As we were leaving, I shouted silently, without uttering a sound, that she was the kindest, deepest, smartest, funniest, sweetest, most delightfully creative person you could have ever met, but you do not deserve to meet her! For her I stayed silent as we went home to her lovely orchids, leaving their apathy behind.

Tiger Orchid In Blue Vase

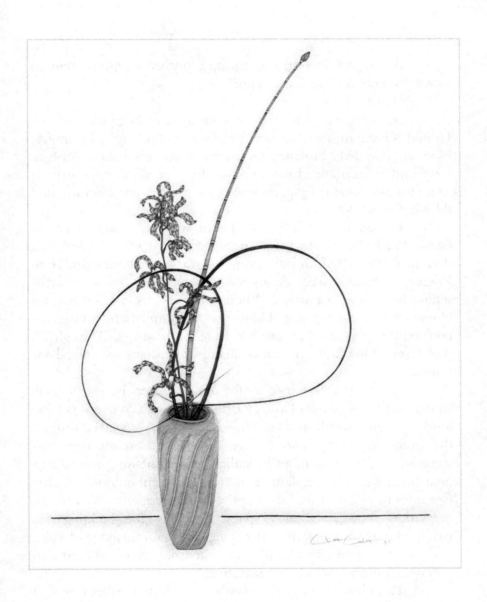

35
Dancing Into Communist Party Headquarters

Before my first trip to Europe, my traveling companion asked, "Where do you want to go?"

"Everywhere!"

So we charted a thirteen country trip beginning in the United Kingdom, then France, Belgium, Netherlands, Denmark, Norway, Sweden, Finland, Germany, Czechoslovakia, Austria, Italy, and Switzerland. I was curious about everything—every art museum, the local people, regional food, varied architecture, and different countrysides.

I wanted to see it all! There was only one place, in particular, I felt certain I had to go because it was so vivid in a dream. I researched and discovered it was the Charles Bridge in Prague, Czechoslovakia. As soon as we got there, I saw an artist selling his prints to tourists. When our eyes met, we felt like we already knew each other. There was an immediate mysterious connection, perhaps because we were both artists. Though he was Czechoslovakian, he spoke fluent English as we talked for hours.

Later, his wife joined us for dinner. After dinner, he took us to another place full of happy drinking people. When it got too loud, we went outside and continued talking as we walked around the grand old city. The variety of elegant architecture was stunning, while the number of stalled reconstruction projects was heartbreaking. He explained it was a combination of the Communist takeover and the apathy of the residents. As a result, everything moved at a slug's pace. Building after building was wrapped in scaffolding, most decaying, many on the edge of ruin. This once elegant city was like an exiled old queen in torn and tattered clothing—stately but suffering.

The citizens seemed as broken down as the buildings. It was clear the system was not working. Our new friend said his family had been on a waiting list for a one-bedroom apartment for years. The faces of the local people in the streets showed resignation. Only the tourists smiled, made noise, or looked happy. A group of Spanish students were singing and playing a game. Our new friend was disturbed by this and said we have to get away from them. I could see he was frightened by the idea of them drawing attention and the Communist guards showing up. It made me sad that these innocent students could attract danger because they were having fun.

We returned to talking of uplifting things, like his love of windsurfing and my love of dancing on roller skates. He asked for a demonstration, and we arranged to meet the next day in a big park. He led us to a wide paved sidewalk in the middle of open fields. I put on my headphones and dance music and showed him dance skating. For a few minutes, I felt carefree, like in Golden Gate Park in San Francisco, where I danced with lots of people, skating, biking, skateboarding, and watching. But here I noticed that even the children did not look. They had never seen such a thing as dance skating in the park before, but still, they showed no interest. The passing people were clearly too scared to hesitate, turn their heads, or draw any attention to themselves. I then realized how oppressive the government was and how much fear the people lived with. How much freedom I take for granted. I felt their pain, and righteous indignation welled up inside. I tried not to show my anger toward how the people were living under the regime because he had to live with it while I got to leave.

After we parted, we were so preoccupied with all the emotions this experience brought up that we accidentally drove into the Communist party headquarters parking lot right around the corner. Two guards with their hands on their machine guns immediately approached the driver's side of the vehicle where my male traveling companion was sitting. They demanded, "Dokument," and kept repeating this seeing the German license plate on our rental car. Every hotel gives its visitors passes and keeps their documents when they check in as collateral until they pay their bill and check out. From where we were, we could all see the Boat Hotel sign that matched our passes. We kept pointing to it and showing them our passes, they just kept repeating "Dokument," louder and louder, even though they knew we did not have them.

I let him deal with them until my rage about how hostile and disrespectful they were toward us and the enormous oppressive way they treated the people there came to the surface, and I said, matching their volume, "You know perfectly well we do not have our documents. We are tourists, and the hotel always takes your documents and gives you these passes that we are showing you. You can see the hotel sign from here. You think because you have machine guns, you can treat people any way you like, but you are just a couple of bullies with bullets. It is wrong the way you have broken the spirits of the people that live here. And you will not do that to me. Back up and let us pass. Now!"

Perhaps because I was speaking English without an accent, or maybe because I was not intimidated by them, or no woman had ever spoken to them like this before, especially one wearing roller skates, as I had not yet taken them off, they backed away laughing.

We drove back to our boat hotel silently. I realized I needed to leave this Communist country before I ran into guards with machine guns that did not find my refusal to be bullied amusing.

The next day as we drove to the border into Austria, the border guard checked our trunk and then opened the back door of our car and put his knee into the cushion with enough force to break the bones of anyone we might be smuggling out under the seat. As happy as I was to be leaving, I was equally sad for all those who had to stay.

Of all the beautiful scenes, classic architecture, kind people, inspirational art, and interesting events in the thirteen countries we visited, this experience went the deepest. I knew I would never take freedom for granted again after accidentally skate dancing into party headquarters.

Dancing Lines Tango

36

Woman Who Dreamt She Was Sleeping But Is Really Light Dancing

On a vision quest, I climbed up the tallest hill in the high desert to fast on the top of it in solitude for three days. I brought only water, matches, a teacup, a sleeping bag, a plastic tarp, rope, a hammock, toilet paper, a pencil, a journal, and a few power bars just in case.

The first night, I found a sheltered spot not far from the top and leveled the earth under the branches. I stretched the rope between the trees and put the plastic over it and the sleeping bag underneath it. I built a small fire and heated water in the teacup.

I sat close to the fire, thinking about the only thing I knew I wanted to do on my vision quest. I wanted to let all sadness and struggle go, so I decided I would write down everything I felt hurt by and everyone who disappointed me. Many things brought up tears with painful memories, which I let run their natural course. It took hours. The only certainty I had was I wanted to be thorough, with nothing important left off the list. My list grew as the day passed with nothing to distract me from feeling each hurt. Drinking my warm water was comforting and satisfying. As I walked away from my camp to relieve my bladder, I experienced the only loneliness I felt during my vision quest. While I was crouching, I said out loud, "I need a friend." Just then a tiny iridescent hummingbird appeared right in front of my face hovering in mid-air. It looked into my eyes with no fear, and I looked into its eyes with great gratitude. It stayed until I stood up. Then it flew a foot away and came back and looked me in the eyes again, and I said, "Thanks little friend. I'm good now," and it flew away. I giggled and returned to the fire.

Sitting on the soft earth, I finished my writing. I decided to read the list out loud and let nature surround me as a sacred witness. Crumpling the sheets of paper, I put them in the fire, and they ignited. As they burned, I said a spontaneous prayer. "Let the fire purify these hurt feelings. Let the winds spread it so far there is no heat left in them anymore." Just as I said this, I watched my perfectly level teacup lift straight up off the ground and move sideways until it was over the center of the fire. Then it turned upside down, extinguishing the fire. I laughed and got into my sleeping bag, pulled it up under my chin, and slept peacefully.

On the morning of the third day, I moved to the top of the tallest hill. There, I collected fallen branches for a big fire. I wanted to keep warm and awake through the night on that last night. I gathered stones for my vision quest circle to enter before the sun went down knowing I wanted to stay within it until the sun came up again. After I put enough fallen branches next to the stones to keep my fire going through the night, I strung up my hammock and laid in it for the rest of the day. Having not eaten for three days and knowing I wanted to stay awake all night, I decided to move as little as possible. I felt comfortable with the big empty spaces between my thoughts. Watching the gray clouds dance around the sky all day, it occurred to me late in the day that I had not asked for my vision quest name yet. So for the first time since I asked for a friend and thanked the hummingbird, I spoke. "What is my name?"

Immediately, a voice came into my head and said, "Woman who dreamt she was sleeping but is really light dancing."

I laughed long and loud at my name and thought, of course, I could not have a name like Babbling Brook, Skipping Deer, or Soaring Crane. Then I had a serious thought, wondering if it was really my name. I decided to say it aloud to find out. I said, "Woman who dreamt she was sleeping but is really—." Just then, the clouds parted for the first time all day as I said, "light dancing," and the sun shone directly on my face as I reclined in the hammock, and I knew it was my name.

As dusk gathered around me, I placed the stones in a circle as I named who each stone represented. The last two stones represented me and me observing myself, which I placed last from inside the circle I would stay in until dawn.

I started a small fire and placed the wood where I could reach it from my sleeping bag. As the darkness increased, so did the stars. I was amazed at the number of stars I could see as I watched the sky all night. Then the shooting stars began. I thought the reason I saw so many shooting stars was because I had not watched the sky until dawn in the high desert before. Later, I was told it was a meteor shower. Wishing on every single one of them kept me busy. I started with huge wishes: world peace, end to hunger, pollution, racism, sexism, elitism, ageism, and illnesses. Then I wished that everyone would find a sense of purpose, love, and joy. As the stars kept shooting, I had to wish as fast as I could, and I started wishing for things for myself, to be able to spin thirteen times on skates, and to get my art published. To keep up with the pace of the streaking lights in the sky, my wishing had to become stream of consciousness.

In an attempt to stay awake, I laid my head on the end of a stick with the other end in the fire. It did keep me awake, not wanting to fall into the flames. It was difficult for the first few hours, but then energy came into me and kept me alert without effort. I wondered why I had not ever chosen to simply observe the night pass into the day in silence before.

After sunrise, picking up the last stone, I left the circle the same way I had come into it. The stones were everyone I had discovered, abandoned, tormented, pleased, dismissed, accepted, feared, respected, teased, taught, learned from, lost, loved—all of my ancestors and angels. There, on a high desert plateau, those stones had watched over the valleys and peaks for eons. I left them there to continue their vigil without me. I walked away weightless, free from blame, resentment, anger, or fear. I had set every burden down. Every doubt had slipped away. Every concern had evaporated. I was empty. I was full. I understood what was essential. It was not good to have a mother who lived compassion, nor was it bad to have a father who lived revenge. I was just born into the time and place I was born into, and what matters is what I do with it.

I set down judgments, hopes, fears, expectations, burdens, desires, disappointments, and triumphs. My struggles are not interesting. Only how I transform them matters. Being born human is an opportunity; let me not squander it. Empty of hurt, full of hope, I removed the last stone and set it aside to leave the circle. I felt like a woman who dreamt she was sleeping but is really light dancing down the hill back to my life.

Yellow Light In Rust Woods

37
Dancing With Death

My mother did not complain about anything, even about her life-threatening asthma attacks. I do not remember a time when she did not periodically struggle to breathe. She described it as feeling like she was drowning. When she had difficulty, my father would get angry and blame her. My siblings were overwhelmed by fear and would get away from her struggling sounds. There was no one left to help her but me. I remember asking the invisible to please give me courage. I comprehended in order to have the strength to help her, I must not fight the fear of her death, but dance with it. Sometimes, her struggling eyes looked to me for reassurance. I would take her hand and hold it in mine. Taking in a huge breath, I would imagine the oxygen I was taking in passing through me into her. With each inhale, I would focus on bringing in peace, and with each exhale, I imagined fear leaving. I would push out the end of each breath and empty my lungs so they would fill effortlessly. She would begin to follow my breathing, and I would nod and smile. Each inhale a little deeper, each exhale was a little bigger. She and I would get more and more relaxed together. I would say what she would have said. "It's going to be alright."

This dance with death my mother and I would do sometimes happened at home or in the car, at a cafe, in an ambulance, or in an emergency room. The doctors and nurses would check in on us periodically, but often they did not even enter the room. They seemed to understand we were doing something the drugs could not do. At those times, she became my child, and I became her mother. It was an honor to give back a little of the tremendous support and love she gave me. During long illnesses, it was exhausting, but I did not ever resent it. It was my privilege to be there for her during her times of vulnerability.

Then, while living with me in San Francisco, she had a coronary and respiratory failure on the city bus. For the first time, the doctors would not let me be with her. I felt helpless, so I did what I felt she would want me to do. I got out a big piece of paper, and I put it on an easel. Putting my colored pencils next to me, I forced myself to stand before the emptiness of the blank paper. It reminded me of our separation, and tears welled up in my eyes. I wanted to fall to my knees and weep. Instead, I said, "For you, dear mother," and I picked up turquoise, coral, yellow, purple, green, maroon, and red colored pencils. Moved by some inexplicable force, my hand drew a gently curving line. One at a time, each color danced across the paper. I gently filled out the lines, widening and thinning, curving and bending. Then brightly colored dots appeared on the page as if someone else was drawing them. This vibrant drawing was like nothing I'd ever drawn before. It was joyous with a carefree simplicity. How much it moved delighted me. I knew it would please my mother, and I felt happy. As I worked, my serenity increased. Whenever I stopped, anxious thoughts crept back into my mind, so I pushed on.

The doorbell rang, and for the first time, my older sister had come to be with me. She never stopped pacing, smoking, and talking. She swung wildly between terror and anger. It gave her comfort that I was calm for a few minutes, then she started to criticize me. I kept drawing, and she turned her anger on me, saying, "How can you draw at a time like this? Don't you feel anything?"

I responded in a quiet voice, saying, "Actually, I feel a tremendous amount. I am drawing to try to stay positive—the only way I can help Mom from a distance."

My sister took a drag of her cigarette and blew it in my direction and stormed out of the room, saying, "I'm going out to get a drink."

The next day the doctor allowed me to see my mother. I brought the drawing I did the night before and set it where she could see it, and I told her I named it Dancing Lines. She loved it. When I picked her up from the hospital the next day, she asked if we could go to Golden Gate Park. She said what she wanted to do more than anything else was sit on a bench in the sun and watch me dance on skates. When I spun, she looked weightless. As I glided by, I could see she was free of gravity. Joyous in the moment, we were alive once again dancing with death.

Star Nebula

38
The Light That Simmers At The Edge Of Everything

My mother did not learn to swim but wanted to face her fear of being in the water. She asked me to sprinkle her ashes at sea and celebrate her transformation, not mourn her death. At her memorial I wore white to honor her wishes. I brought baskets of fresh flowers so everyone could drop lots of color and tender blooms into the water as she would have loved. Then I poured her fine, dove-gray ash onto the bed of multi-colored petals. Her union with the ocean meant she would evaporate and rain down on us. She would join rivers and lakes and flow all around us, comforting us forever.

A sudden gust of wind blew, and I was covered by her ashes. I could not imagine brushing her ash off of me, so I turned and asked, "Who will brush my mother from me?"

My most elderly friend Jonathan Rice answered, "That will take a lifetime."

When we toasted her liberation with a glass of champagne as she asked me to do, a salmon jumped off the bow. Filled with the sweetness of her freedom, my own loss was eased. Watching the roses, irises, and daisies bounce on the gentle sea, I felt her buoyancy, and my heaviness dissolved.

Watching the flowers bounce on the gentle sea, I felt her ever-present steady love, unrelenting forgiveness, and free-flowing joy. I did not know death could be so sweet. I had not imagined the powerful loveliness that fills everything as death moves a loved one out of view. Life came so much closer when her body got further away. Color became more vivid, the stars came nearer, every rustle of a leaf became a song, tenderness filled everything, and clarity replaced confusion. I had not anticipated the great beauty that informed everything as death moved my mother out of my earthly reach.

Mother—you are what a mother is supposed to be: unconditional love, wisdom, kindness, playfulness, forgiveness, guidance, understanding, patience, humor, and compassion. I have been so blessed you are my mother, giving me everything I need. You will always be my ally, teaching me giving is receiving. Thank you for being as proud of my accomplishments as you were your own and for living what you believed.

Thank you for leaving me surrounded by your love. You will never be forgotten. I will try to pass on to others what you gave me—a safe place. Your legacy of love will continue forever, as I pass it on to others, who will pass it on to others. This is immortality, paradise, life after death.

Thank you for showing me my light, for encouraging me to let it shine and to find the courage to share it with others. Thank you for the note, asking, "Did you know you have inner incandescence, dear?" May I shine even the smallest amount of your beautiful brilliance. When you were alive, dear mother, I only heard your voice when you spoke. Now I hear your voice anytime I listen. I used to only see you when you were there. Now you are the light that shimmers at the edge of everything.

Serenity Pond

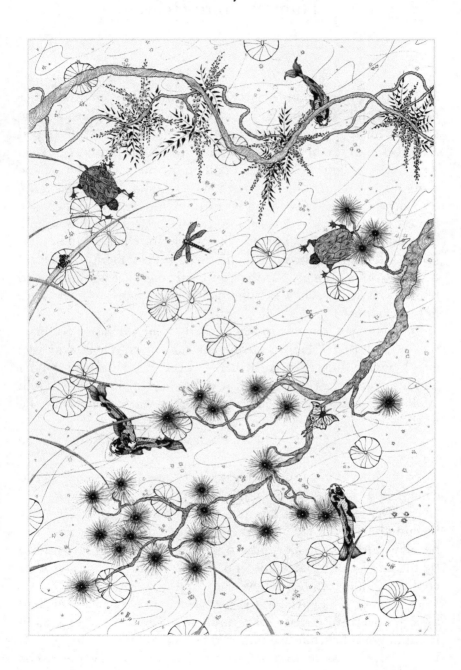

39
Hummingbird Heart

I awoke remembering a vivid dream of a woman with her two small children clinging to a steep, muddy mountainside. The children held on desperately as the waterlogged earth slipped away beneath them. The woman had no expression on her face. There was no light in her eyes. I laid on my belly at the top of the mountain, reaching down to them. The woman did not reach up. She appeared to have already surrendered to the destructive forces. Perhaps she understood if she moved, they would all fall. The children stretched as far as they could to reach my hands. As soon as I grabbed their tiny hands and pulled them to safety, I turned to the woman, but the wet earth had already enveloped her. It was as if she was not holding them up, but they were holding her up.

The next day, my brother called saying our sister Kathryn was in the hospital. Her fourteen-year-old son, who lived with me, and I booked tickets to go to her. I called her older son, who I had also raised but moved out at eighteen. I invited him to join us. I said, "This may be your last chance to forgive her while she is still alive."

Her older son replied, "She does not deserve to be forgiven."

"But you do not deserve to carry this hurt in your heart, even if that is true." He did not join us.

My mother and I watched over her sons from the very beginning as best we could. After years of court battles, my sister never wanted to win but only to fight, I was given guardianship by the court, and that battle ended. But she had so many other conflicts that her path was never peaceful.

When we arrived at the intensive care unit, her heart had already been restarted twice and was beating as fast as a hummingbird heart at two hundred beats a minute.

Her son's questions stunned the doctors who seemed to be used to people viewing death approaching in silent shock. He touched and examined his mother's body with loving scrutiny. He asked, "Why is her skin so gray? Why is there no light in her eyes? Why is her heart beating so fast?" Before the doctor could answer, he continued, "Mom, why didn't you take better care of yourself? Please don't go! God, don't take her. You already took my grandmother!" He wept, and I held him while my brother stood silently by.

Then I said, "Big sister, I wish it had not been so hard for you. I don't blame you for your pain. I've always wanted to say this, but you would not let me. I've always loved you, and I know you always loved me. You only pretended we were enemies." I wept, and he held me as my brother stood without moving or making a sound. "I wish we could have been friends. I know you appreciate me giving your sons a safe home. You can trust I'll watch over them. They are good and kind, and they are gifts you brought into this world. Thank you." My nephew wept, and we held each other. My sister's chest rose and dropped to the rhythm of the machine. Air being drawn into her lungs was not an act born from her will to live; it was simply mechanical. It was clear it was not her life pulsing in her veins. She had already become part of something mysterious. Her body lay without her spirit in it. It was unnatural forcing her unwilling body to live. It felt wrong, so I said what no one wanted to say, which had often been my place in the family, "She is not here anymore. Let her go. Let her be at peace now."

The doctors agreed and explained the drug was what was keeping her heart beating. They said the drug was so powerful it could keep even a heart disconnected from a body beating. They suggested stopping the drug and letting her heart come to a natural stop. My brother agreed with one silent nod. Her son said, "Grandma, take good care of my mom. She is coming to be with you now."

We watched the machine mark her fading pulse as her heart gradually surrendered for the third and final time. We emptied everything left in our hearts as my brother's silence remained unbroken. "Goodbye, Mom. Be at peace now."

I said, "Finally, you can be the big sister you always wanted to be and watch over us all." Her son and I wrapped up in the warmth of each other's arms like small creatures facing the cold.

"Mom, even though you could not always show it, I know you always loved me, and I loved you always too."

I said, "Thank you for not being easy on me. It made me stronger. Know your suffering was not in vain. Your torment inspired my quest for peace. We all learned so much from you. I wish there had not been so much pain for you, but it taught me how important joy is."

Our tears synchronized with her diminishing heartbeat. As her life faded away, so did our fear and resentment. I felt as if my big sister was watching. I wondered if seeing her body so ravaged by the relentless storms of her life would be difficult or no longer mattered. Would it be hard for her to see her body like a discarded vessel tossed ashore, battered and broken? I felt she accepted everything now. I sensed her viewing the scene with forgiveness. This made the hospital, drugs, machines, and strangers all transform into something beautiful.

For the first time since we entered the hospital room, I noticed the room was filled with the softened faces of the nurses, doctors, and technicians gathered around us. This place where so many passed from life to death must have witnessed so much transformation. I could see they were moved by what was taking place. Her son and I gave each other the courage to resolve all our anguish and find forgiveness. We held each other, which gave us the strength to face all that was unresolved and the grief, and arrive at serenity. So many years of suffering my sister had endured and, at times, tried to pass to others, now in minutes transformed into acceptance. So much confusion turned into compassion. In those moments, all the torment evaporated, and nothing but love remained. Even the priest who had come to give their blessing did not speak. The only noise was the machine making its final piercing sound. Her hummingbird heart slowed until it accepted the stillness of death, as we did.

Months after my sister's death I wrote this, and moments after I finished it, the phone rang. It was my brother calling to say what he never had before, "I have been stuck in the grief over our sister's death." I was relieved he could finally speak of it, and hopefully, acceptance and healing would follow.

I understood then what I had suspected. It is not just my story, it is our story—the human story. We are all connected, and when any of us tell our story, it is everyone's story we tell.

Australian Grebe

40 Part I
Waiting Is Worth Waiting For

Twenty years, five months, and fourteen days ago, I watched my son, like a butterfly, emerging from its cocoon. For him to fly, I had to let go. Every day since that day, I have waited willingly for this day. Waiting can be worth waiting for, simply because it is the right thing to do.

Since his birth, separation is the only thing we have shared. We have never heard each other's laugh, looked into each other's eyes, known each other's cry, but we know each other. Love crosses all time instantly and spans any distance without effort.

The place my love for him lives is uncluttered with none of the details of everyday living. The space where love lives is simple and free. There, all things are reduced to their essence the way death makes all but love insignificant.

For inexplicable reasons, I knew it was time to find him. I felt it without doubt that all the time waiting was worth waiting for, and this was the moment. I went to a search person who found his name the same day. I went home and found his phone number, and I called immediately. When I heard what I felt certain was his voice, I hung up without saying anything. I felt it was the right time for me to find him but not the right time to reach out to him. I waited another seven months wanting to call every day, but I knew it was not the time for him.

I spoke to many people who had adopted or been adopted. But no one who had given up a child for adoption shared their experience with me. Everyone had a different opinion, and everyone believed their opinion was correct. They all offered advice like, let someone else call him, have a lawyer write him, go knock on his door, write a letter, call his parents, tell him not to tell his parents, don't contact him at all. One man in his eighties who had adopted a son, and was adopted himself, was the only one who said, "Your patience will be rewarded."

I felt everyone's approach could be right for some situations. But this was me, my son, and his parents. I listened to everyone but knew I would not do anything until it felt right in my heart and head.

What would I say to my son? Is there anything but the truth? Would I start by telling him I gave him away because I loved him, not because I didn't? How would I tell him his father was a man who raped me, creating his life with no regard for either of us. How could I tell him life is strange, sometimes unfair and cruel? Violence can be indiscriminate. Anything can happen, and sooner or later everything will. How could I expect him to believe I have always loved him when he has not heard from me?

I woke from a nap, and I knew it was time. I got his phone number. It had been sitting in a little box on top of my desk since the day I got it. I got a glass of water, a handkerchief, and I sat down deep breathing before I dialed. As the phone rang, my life passed before me, as they say it does just before death. I felt everything I had endured prepared me for this moment.

A young man answered. I asked if he was the first, middle, and unusual last name the hospital records led to.

"Yes," he replied.

"Are you somewhere we can have a confidential conversation?"

"Yes."

"Do you know you are adopted?"

He said, "Yes."

"Well," I paused for a moment, perhaps taking the deepest breath of my life and continued, "I am your birth mother."

"It is great to hear from you!" he said with boyish enthusiasm.

"I have had your number for seven months. I don't know why it felt right to call you today."

"Because the timing is perfect!"

"Why?" I asked.

"My father and I decided last night to find you."

We both felt a serene silence for a while. In those quiet moments, I felt all the time and distance between us was an illusion, and we had always been together. We were connected by the primal wound we shared—a child and mother separated. We were strangers who knew each other intimately. We had never seen each other, but we had also not really been apart. Life is so full of paradoxes. Not knowing what each other looked or smelled like was minuscule compared to the understanding we had of one another. This was my son. I am his mother.

We shared the same body for nine months. We both came from my mother and her mother before her. What we have shared was huge, and the details of what we hadn't seemed small in comparison. We recognize ourselves in one another. He spoke of his dreams and feeling of being in the eye of a hurricane, as I have often described my childhood. He told me about writing poetry, drawing, and loving to move, and I told him I love doing all those things.

I told him that I hung up without speaking when I called seven months earlier because it did not feel like the right time for him.

"You were right. It was not the right time, because I had just gotten in an accident, and I had temporary brain damage, which just healed, so this is the perfect time."

Everything extraneous fell away. I felt so grateful I trusted my instincts and waited until the time felt correct for him. I felt a mysterious assistance. All my fear and doubt evaporated like steam off a hot summer pond. I felt a deeper peace. We were strangers who had once resided within the same body. I felt the tranquility of a mother watching over her peacefully sleeping child. Finally, I did not have to trust my child was all right. I could hear it from him as he said, "The empty place in me has been filled." I felt the same, and finally, I got to wish my son sweet dreams, and we both slept peacefully that night.

The older adopted man who adopted a son was right when he said, "Your patience will be rewarded." And I understood waiting is worth waiting for.

Penguin Contemplating Egg

40 Part II
The Lavender Karate Gi

As they carried my newborn out of the delivery room, I knew I would not see him learn to crawl, speak, walk, throw a ball, or ride a bike. I would have no contact with him. I was barely sixteen when I was raped, and he was conceived. I could not protect him, as all children deserve to be safe. I was not safe. Knowing what I had to do did not make it easier, but it made it possible.

A mother's love can endure whatever it has to for the child, even the excruciating suffering of being separated. It took all my strength I could summon to let him go. I knew I had to as soon as he could breathe on his own, or my resolve may weaken, and that was unacceptable.

My mother did not tell me for years that she held him after he was born. I did not want her to have to bear the pain of separation with me so I told her she should not put herself through that. She always did what she thought was right, which I admired, and I was grateful she was stronger than me. Knowing it would help him to be held and hear he was loved, immediately she rose above selfish suffering to selfless serenity. And she did not tell me, so I would not worry about her.

I had arranged with the county for parents who were able and good people. I came to understand that the attorney I went to did not do background checks on his clients. He would arrange an adoption for anyone who could afford to pay his fee. When I pointed this out to the attorney, he offered me money if I went through him, so I did not return. I went to the county adoption agency, where they checked out the couple to make sure they were safe and capable people.

The first phone conversation with my son filled a dark, cold place with warm light for us both. During our second phone call, we talked of many things before he told me about his dream from the previous night. In the dream, he went shopping for a karate gi with his adoptive mother. He found a purple one and

175

really wanted it, while his adoptive mother tried to talk him out of buying it.

I said, "Right now I am wearing a karate gi that I bought at a used store and dyed lavender. This is the first time I've worn it in years." Neither of us was surprised that somehow we were connected. I asked him, "What were you doing on your last birthday?"

He thought about it and answered, "I just knew I had to get some art, so I went to a poster store and bought *Guernica*, Picasso's painting of a bull."

I responded, "I was traveling in the desert with my family, and I woke up from a nap saying, 'Where is my bull? I know I am supposed to see a bull, and this is the last day. Where is he?' Just then, our vehicle got to the top of a rise where we could see ahead of us for miles and miles, and ahead was one tree with a bull sitting under it. I yelled out, 'There he is!' We stopped next to him and spun the wheels, shooting out pebbles to get him to stand up so I could take a picture. I carved the calico-colored bull into a ceramic vase that stands in my kitchen. I also saw a flock of cranes overhead on that birthday of yours. I celebrate your birthday every year."

He said, "I always felt it. Thanks."

"Whatever you want to do next, I trust you."

He said with surprise in his voice. "You do?"

"Yes, I do."

"My dad wants to talk to you, but my mom will not ever be ready."

His dad got on the phone and said his wife was not able to talk but wanted to listen on the other line.

"That's fine. I waited until your son was twenty, so no one was confused about who his parents are. You two are his parents, I appreciate you both from the bottom of my heart truly. I gave up the right to parent him, but I did not give up the right to love him. I called to tell him that I let him be adopted because I love him, not because I do not."

At that point, I could hear his adoptive mother crying on the other end of the line, and then she said, "I have always wanted to hate you, but I can't because you are too kind, but did you have to be so interesting!"

Trying to comfort her, I said, "I used to be a janitor," realizing later it just made me more interesting.

After his parents got off the phone, my son and I agreed it was time to see each other. With the blessing of his parents, I flew down the next day. He suggested we meet at the South Coast Plaza by the carousel.

As I entered, I saw my son across the vast space. I recognized him immediately even though I had not seen him since his birth, and the only photo the adoption agency sent me was when he was an infant.

We walked across the plaza to one another and held each other for the first time. Neither of us wanted to let go. Perhaps we never would have if the desire to look into one another's eyes had not been so strong. We understood at that moment that not a day had passed without being in each other's lives. Our love had connected us. Knowing each other passed through time and distance unaltered. Love cannot be contained. It is without form and cannot be halted by anything physical. It passes through all obstacles without hesitation and travels through time and over any distance unaffected by worldly realities. Love exists of itself and for itself. I believe it may be the most potent force in the universe. It offered us hope during those times when a mother and child who had been separated have nothing else but their love that cannot be extinguished.

Without knowing any of his details, I knew him. His life was unfamiliar, but I knew his essence. I comprehended him without knowing any of the particulars of his day-to-day life. As we spoke, I saw myself in his deep, stormy eyes. His eyes were lit from the inside as people have said of mine. I suggested we go outside of the mall to be under the stars. I felt that even the enormously high ceilings in the mall could not contain the expanse of our feelings.

We talked about many things, and finally, I asked, "What do you know about your father?"

He answered that the adoption agency sent him one letter, and it said his mother was an artist, and his father was a college student, and they were too young to raise a child. Then he added, "But I knew it was not true."

"What did you think was true?" I asked.

He answered, "I used to hate you for giving me away, but then I realized he was the one I should hate."

"Why do you hate him?"

"Because he forced me on you and abandoned us both."

"Why do you think this? What have you been told?"

He said, "Nothing other than the one letter the adoption agency sent me, but I felt it. I knew. I used to have rape dreams, and I figured it out."

I did not know what to say. I did not deny it or confirm it. But my silence said it all.

We were strangers who had once resided within the same body. As he spoke of dreams and feelings, I heard myself in him. Everything extraneous fell away in those moments, and only our spirits stood before each other. All things were beautiful and illuminated, even the brutality of his conception transformed into the gift of life. We understood that we had always been wrapped in the strong softness of each other's love like the mysterious lavender karate gi.

Praha Prague

41
Bodhi Is Born

If I wished to get pregnant, I would have to take hormones, gain weight, and stop dancing the doctors said. I decided to leave it up to the wisdom of my body and go on a retreat in Mexico. The place that had been empty since parting with my newborn could now be filled after finding my first son and telling him I arranged his adoption because I loved him, not because I didn't.

When I saw a big, beautiful pregnant woman on the beach, I felt my fertility return. I celebrated by going for a long swim after the locals assured me the waters were safe. I swam for an hour in the bay over to the next beach La Ropa and back. I had a habit of trying to pick up my pace during the swim back to see how fast I could go. As I walked out of the ocean totally spent, I had an odd feeling that made me look back at the water. Under the waves I saw a huge, dark shape that I could not make out. The fisherman who was standing waist high in the water close to where I came ashore suddenly jumped out of the ocean and yelled something in Spanish to the two men in a small fishing boat just past the breakers. They grabbed a gaffing hook and stuck it in the water and pulled something out that immediately shook loose and disappeared. I did not have any idea what it was, and the fisherman on the shore disappeared before I could ask him. And the two in the boat motored off as quickly. I wondered if, in this tourist economy, they had done something they didn't want to speak of.

The next morning on a break-of-dawn walk, I saw a twelve-foot crocodile with a gash under its lower jaw dead on the beach. The locals cleared it off within minutes of sunrise. I had no idea crocodiles could live in saltwater. If I had seen it while I was in the water swimming in the bay from one beach to the other, I don't know if I would have been able to maintain my composure and not panic and swallow water. Standing in a sad sort of shock looking at the mortally wounded creature, I wondered how long it had been following me.

"Why didn't it eat me?" I asked a man who said he lived in Florida, where there are lots of salties.

He answered, "Don't worry. Crocs prefer dead meat. I've seen them take a cow off the shore, kill it, and leave it there and come back to eat it later."

I snapped, "Oh, that is comforting! So I shouldn't worry because it would have only killed me, not eaten me but then left me there for my young nephew to find my torn up body." I stomped away, deciding losing my enjoyable swim in the bay was better than losing my life to a crocodile, whether it wanted to eat me now or later.

Returning home, I went to the doctor who confirmed I was pregnant. It was great news. Since I'd been parenting my older sister's boys on and off since I was seventeen, I did not think I wanted to raise another, but it filled me with joy. To be able to leave the hospital with him instead of alone was so healing. To start at the beginning with a baby instead of trying to repair the damage caused by someone else's abuse and neglect felt like a sublime gift.

At seven months pregnant, my son's father suggested the name Bodie, the name of a ghost town in the Sierras. I said it out loud, and my baby jumped inside of me as if recognizing his name. I like to find something to honor in each spiritual tradition, and the Jewish custom of naming a child after the first initial of a loved one felt right. Barbara, my beloved mother, and Bodhi, my beautiful son. I said it, and again he jumped, and it felt like he recognized his name. I spelled Bodhi after the tree, not the ghost town. Later, I heard that Buddha reached enlightenment under the Bodhi Tree.

I checked into the hospital the night before my early morning cesarean. A nurse washed a different newborn baby outside my room every hour all night long without closing the door to my room. Every squealing infant woke me. I was not allowed to eat or drink anything since checking in to the hospital. Cesareans are rated at the same level of trauma as open heart surgery, but since women have them as part of motherhood, they are given little consideration. When they brought me into the surgery room that was forty-five degrees to prevent bacteria from growing, it took everything I had not to shiver while bending forward as the anesthetic needle was inserted into my spine. The drug allowed me to be lucid so I could be there for the birth of my son. Feeling everything, but not registering it as pain was strange, but I was conscious, which was important to me.

He was taken from my womb and to a table where they checked him, saying he was fine. The doctor, assistant, and his father were gushing about how beautiful he was.

I said, "Can I see him?" My arms were tied down to prevent me from moving while they were performing the surgery, so I could only nuzzle him with my face. When I said his name, he opened his eyes.

Before going into the hospital, I felt I needed to be prepared, so I did something I had never done before. I assigned different answers to playing cards. I shuffled them and asked specific questions about the next few days. The answers revealed my son would appear to have trouble that would pass in three days. So when they told me he had moisture in his lungs, which could be pneumonia, I felt sure it was not, but in an abundance of caution, I let them take him to the nursery to be safe.

Being separated from him was excruciating. We had been in the same body for nine months, feeling every movement the other made. Always in contact and in essence, moving as one. First, they took me to the recovery room. It was very surreal because I could not think about my legs. It was as if I was not connected to them. Slowly, I was able to sense them and move them again, and they took me back to my room. I had never been so tired, and I wanted to sleep, but I could not without seeing my son. Only once in my life have I ever gotten hysterical, but I felt it was possible now, which I told my son's father. He was looking at his phone messages and offered no comforting words. Perhaps he did not take me seriously because he had never seen me lose my composure.

I was scared and exhausted, I closed my eyes and asked the ineffable for help. Immediately, I felt myself leave my body

182

and float above the bed. Then out of the room and down the hall to the right. Then another right, another long, narrow, gray-walled hall where I had not been before. Then I took a third right turn, and in a short distance I came to a window into an office next to an open door where a rotund, feminine black man was sitting behind a desk working at a computer. He did not see me as I floated past him into the nursery room. The rectangular room was full of clear plastic incubators with newborn babies in them. Two nurses were talking, and they did not notice me. As I knew I was floating over to Bodhi's incubator, out of the corner of my eye I saw some commotion the nurses did not see. Turning to see what it was, I saw my mother in a bright flowered dress, getting my attention by waving her arms in the air. Though my mother died years before Bodhi was born, she was there. I could see tiny glistening beads of sweat on her face.

She communicated with me without sound, "I am watching over Bodhi. Get back in your body, dear. You need your rest."

Instantaneously, I was back in my body in my hospital bed, where Bodhi's father was still looking at his phone.

I said, "I am okay," and he went home.

The next morning when he came to visit, I told him what happened last night.

He said, "You must have seen it in a movie." After he went to see Bodhi and saw everything I described as I had described it—even though he knew I had not been there yet—he said nothing.

Some people can only accept what they can explain. Other people can experience mysterious things that have no explanation. Like when Bodhi was five, and a retreat guest in our home asked him, "Is there significance to you being named Bodhi?"

Bodhi stared at the man for a long silence. The man appeared to be in a state of grief, so I bent down and whispered to Bodhi, "I think he needs to hear some words from you."

Then Bodhi said in a matter-of-fact tone, while still looking directly into the man's eyes, "There's a bodhisattva in the world." The man's mouth fell open, and Bodhi lifted his hands and said, "Duh!"

The man laughed for the first time in days.

Later, I asked Bodhi, "What is a bodhisattva?"

He answered, "They stay to help people."

"Where did you learn that?"

"I read it at the Asian Art Museum."

Raising Bodhi has been joyous. He was content, secure, and happy from the very beginning. An older man friend referred to him as the baby who never cried. How simple it seems to give a child what they need, and yet many do not get the essentials. If I could make a wish for the world, it would be that everyone is cared for.

A bodhisattva is a person who can ascend to nirvana but delays doing so out of compassion to assist other suffering beings. I did not know Bodhi meant a person of great knowledge until years after he was born.

When he was five, he wanted to have a stand for the hikers who passed our house. He asked, "What can I sell?"

I said, "Bottled water, lemonade, popcorn, cookies." He was not happy with those suggestions, so sarcastically, I said, "What about spiritual advice."

He asked, "What is that?"

I said, "It is when people have questions about life."

"Like what?"

"Like, what will make me happy?"

"I don't know. If you think something will make you happy, try it. What else would they ask?"

"How will I find love?"

"Sometimes you find the girl, and sometimes she finds you. One more question."

So I thought I should ask a good one and said, "What is the greatest strength a person can have?"

He thought for a minute, "To just walk away from your enemies."

I wondered, does my son carry my mother's wisdom? Everyone who knew my mother would describe her as a bodhisattva. Is my son carrying this lineage? Am I the conduit of my mother to my son? Are we all born enlightened but lose touch with what we are born knowing?

I may never have answers to these or other most important questions: Where does life come from? How did we gain the ability to contemplate it? Is there a god, goddess, both, one, or many? Was it a singularity that began the universe, or multiverse, or something we cannot imagine that is the origin of life? Questions fill me. Answers elude me. The ineffable surrounds us all. I am content with the mystery. Love may be the most powerful force in the universe. The love between mother and child is divine. I have no words to describe the depth of my gratitude that Bodhi was born.

South African Cranes In High Nest

42 Part I
Raining In The Monastery

Outside the window, silver olive trees follow the roll of the Italian hills. An aura of salmon pink clouds glows at the mountain's edge. Brilliant white snow dusts the highest peaks. Terra-cotta villas dot the landscape. I am sitting on an enormous bed in this thousand-year-old carved stone monastery as the golden dusk is fading while darkness wraps me in cool stars.

No longer lured out the window, I am drawn into my own invisible interior. I have come here to write without distractions. As I begin, a sense of awesome responsibility comes over me. The weight of wondering, what do I have to say, is so heavy. Sharing my life without sensationalizing my struggle is daunting. I feel angry at my imaginary audience wanting to hear the difficult things I've been through. Then I realize the act of sharing isn't for others—but an act of love toward myself. If I do not tell my story, how will I ever truly know myself? I feel sharing my truth can transform my pain into purpose, helping me by helping others. Giving is also receiving.

As I consider writing my stories, I recall the day years ago when nine different people told me I should teach dance. Now I understand that those who say I should write know something I do not yet comprehend. Back then, those who suggested I teach creative movement saw something in me I did not yet see in myself.

I kept resisting, saying, "But I've not studied dance. What do I know?"

They said, "You know how to dance." I gave them the respect of accepting they knew something I did not, and it changed my life for the better. Teaching was a gift that expanded me beyond myself. Service is a sort of freedom. Every time I went to the psychiatric hospital exhausted and danced with suffering people, I was invigorated. When I reached deep inside to help another, I found rewarding purpose and peace there.

Now I am no longer thinking about whether it is a curse or a blessing to have an interesting life full of challenges. It is not what I have been given that makes me who I am; it is what I do with what I have been given that defines me. It is not good or bad to have lived these things, but sharing it to know myself better and help others is good.

It is my choice to transform my adversity into advantage. So as I begin writing, I recall a visit with a mentor and respected friend that ignited curiosity within me. When Walter Landor, the founder of an international design firm, was in the hospital, he asked to see my art. I brought my portfolio and showed him one piece at a time. As he looked at each one slowly and carefully, he said, "There is a book here. You should tell stories looking at your own art."

So I am including my art in this book in honor of him. Each piece tells a different silent story. His last words to me as I was leaving the hospital that evening were, "Don't put anything off!" Walter had a stroke later that night and did not regain his ability to speak. He and I had spoken many times over the years about his life story book project. He interviewed many people to write his life story, but he could not decide on one, so he passed before it happened later that year.

I heard him and I took the next step by consulting a Greek woman I met on a vision quest who said, "You have something to say."

"What?"

"You have learned forgiveness."

"But I have so much more forgiveness to learn."

"You have humility."

"What about my doubts, fears, and vanity?"

"You are human, and your willingness to feel and express your humanness is what makes you exceptional."

"So being exceptionally human is what I have to share?"

"Yes," she answered, and something within me shifted. I felt intrigued by Walter's idea about looking at my art and telling stories from my life. I was inspired and began days later with my Greek friend holding up one painting at a time. As I looked at each piece as if for the first time, I wrote down the first feeling that came to me: compassion, jealousy, respect, fear, understanding, denial, hope, despair, joy, dread, harmony. . . . This was fascinating, as I felt so many different things when I looked at my art, but everyone who shared what they felt while looking at my art said the same thing, "Peace."

Now in this old monastery that has become my friend's home in Italy, I am continuing my writing journey of self-discovery. Before this time, the very thing I have been ashamed of, how much I feel, how vulnerable I am, how sensitive I am, turns out to be a great gift. The feeling of duty lifts and is replaced by a sense of adventure.

Shall I meander a stream of consciousness path through my past or go on an orderly chronological account of my history? Should I embellish for better stories or stick to the truth no matter how uninteresting? Can I leave out the parts that make me look bad and expand the parts that make me look good and have it still be the truth? Is it for my own evolution, or more importantly what it offers others? How do I know what is meaningful to others? The more I ask these questions, the more overwhelmed I feel. I realize I do not need answers. I need the faith that I have when I dance or paint to let it flow and just get out of the way of the creative expression. There is no right or wrong way. All that is necessary is to do it honestly, not embellish or leave out the unflattering. Simply tell the truth the best I can. Let it flow and be raw and instinctive, and as my mother called my artistic style "elegant primitivism."

After writing this, I fall asleep, and I awake in the middle of the night to rain dripping onto my bed in this thousand-year-old monastery. I go to the kitchen and get pots and cloth napkins to put in the bottom of each pot to keep the dripping sound from keeping me awake, and I go back to sleep soundly.

In the morning, the first thing I see when my eyes open is four of the Portuguese workers and my friend laughing. They are looking at me curled around the seven pots in my bed. One of the house workers asks, "Why didn't you wake me to help you?"

"I figured it out, so I did not need to."

I noticed at breakfast for the first time since my arrival the helpers smiled at me. After they left the dining room, I asked my friend, "They have been so distant until today. What changed?"

She said, "They thought you were a princess, but I told them who you actually are." Until then, they had misunderstood me because I brought my most beautiful clothing, gifts from designer friends and unique items I found in used stores. I delighted in mixing and matching each outfit, not wearing the same ensemble twice. Every meal was meticulously served to us by the staff at a precise time, so I came in a different outfit to honor each meal for the fun of it.

After seeing me asleep curled around the seven pots, and my friend telling them I worked on the boats with the longshoremen, they saw who I really was, the night it rained in the monastery.

Mono Lake

42 Part II
Longing For Belonging

Christine had given me a shaman's book while I was in Italy at her old monastery turned into an olive orchard. I put the book under my pillow, as I often did, instead of reading it. Later, when we were both back in California, she invited me to the shaman author workshop. We flew to New Mexico together. Our white airport van full of weary travelers pulled up to the hot springs outside of Santa Fe, New Mexico. Christine didn't feel well and went home, but her daughter Ilena stayed for the workshop. We enjoyed each other and became instantly close. She was honest and light-hearted, which was a nice fit with my often heavy honesty.

I was nervous my writing would not be as good as the others, and my nerves were made sharper by the fact that this was my first workshop. Wanting to get over my self-consciousness right away, I raised my hand at the first session after all the others willing to read their assignments. The shaman pointed to me and said, "Lady in the back. I don't know who you are, but I recognize souls."

I stood up and looked around the room before speaking. "Thank you for letting me face my fear," then I read my piece inspired by my assigned writing partner's object as we were directed. He brought a polished obsidian stone with flecks of silver about which I wrote:

Light blackness
Womb of worlds
Before the big bang
A minuscule speck
Containing all possibilities
Goddess blinks
Everything
We can imagine
Into existence

"Beautiful poem," the shaman teacher said before he paused and continued, "and it is true," he said, "but you need to get more primitive."

"That's very interesting," I said. "My mother called me the elegant primitive."

"That's probably true, but you still need to get more primitive," he snapped.

After the session, when no one else could hear, the shaman told me I was a poet. I went outside to meet my partner and said, "I feel like I have found my people. But an even greater joy than my sense of belonging is my son feeling safe to share his first poem in school." Bodhi had written a poem for a class assignment, and it had stunned us. My writing partner shared the sweetness of the moment with me. When I went into the hotel lobby, Bodhi's poem I just mentioned was in a fax pinned on the board. It seemed like a perfect offering to the group as a token of appreciation for my feeling of welcome.

After everyone else who wanted to read was done at the end of the day, I said, "I feel this is a gift for the group because of the magical timing of its appearance," and I read my eight-year-old son Bodhi's poem:

Space
It never starts
It never stops
It is full and empty
At the same time
Space is like an adventure
As the world is to me
It is a big nothingness
That grows every day
To me, the stars
Are the fruit
And space is
The tree
I hope to one day
Reach the fruit
And taste its glow
With my eyes.

The room sighed warmly. On my way back to my seat, I felt so comfortable, I said jokingly, "I think I will quit and just let him write."

A woman said, "Be his teacher."

"Yes, and he is my teacher," I replied.

"You should not show appreciation to children. It makes them strange," said a man with a particularly long face. I felt compassion for that man, imagining the childhood he must have had.

"I do not like people who do not shade their children from the direct sun," the shaman hissed.

I wondered why he thought he knew anything about me as a mother. Why has this gift, a delicate flower, turned into a poisonous snake? I had surrendered my shields and stood bare before them, and those who did not like their own image in the reflective surface of my vulnerability shattered my mirror heart. Still water is easily disturbed.

Moments before, I thought I had found someplace I thought I could belong. Then in the next instant, the dancing rainbows on the surface of my bubble burst. I spent my evening in my room, writing:

> Quaking leaf heart
> Blown apart by winds of insecurity
> No matter in the eyes of eternity
> All troubles tiny as a caterpillar's eyelash.

Then I heard the people in the next room as if there were no walls. "She should not have read her child's poem! Who does she think she is?"

I whispered to myself, "Why do I hear these words? What purpose other than to hurt me?" I began to cry and briefly fell asleep. Then I awoke, and wrote in the quiet dark:

> Fear takes sweetness hostage
> Everyone who loses
> Confidence in their worthiness
> Fuels fire of disdain
> Hold tight to convictions
> Let the wind of gossip blow
> Respect your integrity
> Do not feed the desire to contain
> What cannot be contained
> Fear fuels judgment
> Love is the unshakable
> Devotion to kindness.

I thought those who had come to share with strangers would know themselves. They would be trustworthy and ready to be vulnerable. In the morning, I told my new friend Ilena I didn't feel safe with the others, and I was skipping the session to soak in the mineral waters nearby. There I found forgiveness and wrote:

> Stand for something
> Become a target
> Dare to trust
> Be struck down
> Know infinite love
> Be hated
> By those who do not
> Love self
> Go to the
> Well of forgiveness
> Drink waters of welcome
> Love with exiled heart.

In the evening, my partner came to see me and asked me if I was okay. I told him, "I needed to be alone. I heard what they

195

said about me through the walls last night." He looked sad. "It isn't your responsibility. I only told you because I felt bad about abandoning you today. You do not need to do anything." Then we spoke about his mother-in-law's impending death, which made my difficulties seem small in comparison. He decided to tell the others I had overheard everything they had said about me.

While I was eating in the dining room, the two from the next room approached me. As soon as the woman looked into my eyes, she burst into tears and started a fast-talking apology at the same time the man was saying, "I am so sorry. Can you ever forgive me, please?"

I hugged her, saying, "I already have." She pulled back and looked at me astonished.

"You have?"

"Yes, I have."

"God," she continued while her tears increased, "if I had to be such an asshole, I am so glad it was to such a nice person." I was amused by the duality of it all but held back a laugh.

Feeling embarrassed about the public display, I stood and started walking, saying, "Let's talk out there," and they followed.

"It is huge for me. I really needed this lesson," the woman said.

"This is very important for me, too," I said. They both looked startled and confused.

"Why?" the woman asked.

"Because of all the other strangers at other times in my life, who did not know me and spoke cruel things about me, you are the first to apologize."

She looked at me confused and asked, "This has happened before?"

"Yes."

"Because you are so beautiful . . . right?" she asked.

"No," I answered, "because I accept myself."

My partner told me the shaman had asked where I was and then said to the room, "She must be embarrassed she read her son's poem."

When I heard this, I decided to rejoin the group the next day, but not to speak. That evening, the shaman was signing his books. I bought one and got at the end of the line. When I reached him, I said, "Before I ask for the gift of your signature, I would like to offer you a gift." I handed him my book, *Book of Cranes*.

He took it in his hands, looked at the outside briefly, and said, "A feather," and immediately began a conversation with someone else. He slipped the book out of its case, flipped through it quickly, and set it on the floor, saying, "I am not signing any more books tonight." I was the only one still waiting. I picked my *Book of Cranes* up off the floor and left.

Jealousy is much more common than I ever wanted to admit. I have not wanted to speak of it for fear it will make me a target. Truly hard to admit was the shaman was jealous, but he was a human being, more like the rest of us than different.

The second to last night, the shaman was signing posters on the floor. I waited in the back of the room until almost everyone had gone. When only his wife remained in the front with him, I walked up, got down on the floor with him and said, "I'm going to try this again. I'm going to try to give you a gift." I handed him my book while no one else was watching.

He accepted it and said, "It is beautiful."

On the last day of the workshop, the shaman spoke for a long time about jealousy, saying, "I am jealous of poets. They can just tell the truth. I have to drive it, and as Robert Bly says about me, until I drive it around the bend." Then I recalled the shaman telling me I was a poet on the first day.

As I stood the first day and thanked the group for helping me to face my fear, I thought I was speaking about my fear of sharing my writing. I realized then it was the much greater fear of being the object of jealousy and the terrible pain of separation envy puts between people. I have suffered so much anguish because others thought I had something they did not. I know I deserve love, and those who do not know this will hold it against those who do. The irony of it all is I learned to love myself out of necessity—I had so little else growing up. It was born out of disadvantage rather than the privilege others project onto me.

The last day during the shaman's long lecture, he said, "If you are jealous of someone, give them a gift to transform your jealousy."

My new friend Ilena looked at me from across the room and mouthed the words, "You have to get out of here." The moment the lecture was over, I bolted toward the door.

Before I could get through it, a woman jumped in front of me. "You are the most beautiful woman I have seen in . . ." she paused. I wanted to run away, and seeing my discomfort, she finally continued, "in a really long time."

I suggested to Ilena we go to the dining room before the others. As we sat there, five women who had not spoken to me the whole retreat came over and told me I was pretty.

Another said, "Are you a yoga master? I mean, your body. You must be a dancer. Do you teach yoga? You must, because your body, I mean, the way you move. You are a dancer, right? Do you teach dance? Are you a yogi?" She kept talking without giving me an opportunity to answer, which worked out considering I did not know what to say.

Ilena and I whispered after each left our table, "Boy, it is getting really high. It is going to hurt when they knock me off the pedestal they're putting me on!"

The man with the particularly long face approached me and said, "You are a person of enormous grace." Feeling this was a genuine compliment and a gift for me rather than for themselves like the others felt, I thanked him.

After eating, the group walked up the dirt road and got in the white van to go to the airport:

> Poem pure
> Like a flower
> Turned into snake
> Strikes me
> Venom transforms hurt
> Into sweet forgiveness.

When we got back to California, Christine reminded me of the dream I told her while I was visiting her in Italy. The night I slept with the shaman's book under my pillow I dreamt it was

Halloween, but I did not want to dress up. I just wanted to be myself. I went down to the water, and there were two native men, one was feminine and comfortable with me, and the other was masculine and threatened by me. An earthquake came, and I suggested we go out into the water to get away from the rocks at the shore and float through the quake. After the shaking passed, we all walked up the dirt road, got in a white van, and drove away.

I went to the workshop hopeful and longing for belonging. I returned and shared my experience with the family therapist, who had known me for fifteen years. I asked him, "Is it strange I am feeling sad about women telling me I'm pretty? Do you understand why?"

He answered, "I think I do. It is that you have worked your whole life on polishing an inner jewel that they don't even see."

At that moment, my longing for belonging faded into an appreciation of being seen.

Warblers

43 Part I
Heavenly Souvenir On The Vacation To Hell

My father was drawn to places no one else wanted to go. There were good reasons people avoided these places: quicksand, thick thorn bushes, wild boars, unbearable heat, or no water. My father craved extremes. If it was not dramatic, he was not interested. Once, he decided we should vacation on the salt flats that almost swallowed our car in the night. Then there was the time he drove us down to the beach where the high tide line was thirty feet higher than our vehicle. There were many places where we kids had to dig the vehicle out of mud or sand while my father drank beer and barked orders.

There were the rare times my father, for some inexplicable reason, chose a campground. They were the safest trips but still terrible because of his need to be the center of attention at all times. He commanded this attention through different means: his sharp wit, commanding charm, or the public humiliation of his children. It did not matter to him how he got it. In campgrounds, he would perform for the other campers by yelling in a voice no one could ignore, "Okay, kids. Line up three times!"

This translated into the four of us standing shoulder to shoulder in descending order and repeating three times, "Patience, love, and understanding." If we did not say it loud enough for everyone in the campground to hear, he would have us do it over again. This display would satisfy my father's need to stand out for a short time, and it would cause me to hide from the other campers in embarrassment. I preferred the peril of wild adventures to that humiliating display.

My task was fire maker, which was the best part of any trip. While out gathering wood, I could enjoy nature and quiet. Bringing light and warmth to the camp was a protection from my father's darkness. I would go in ever-widening circles, observing the land and its creatures, getting all the companionship I needed from the tiny silent beings. The distant stars and the endless expanse made all my troubles feel minuscule. I cherished the calm. As I filled my arms with wood, my heart filled with the serenity of the wild places. I wrapped the natural world around me like a warm blanket. The stillness became my shield.

Part of my father respected me for finding a way to keep out of the reach of his pain. Part of him resented me for the invisible distance I put between us. We all lived at the foot of the volcano that was my father, never knowing when his rage would erupt and incinerate everything in its path. He survived on chaos, while I thrived on peace. I accepted our differences and that we may never truly understand each other. He did not know how I thought. I did not know what he felt. My love for him did not depend on comprehending him. He was my father. My love for him occurred naturally. It simply existed past all the pain he was in and the anguish he passed on to others.

Years later, my brother decided to organize the only trip since our childhood on Father's Day weekend. He said our father would be joining us. When my partner said he would like to come along, I said, "Before you decide, I need to tell you how I survived my childhood."

"How?" he asked.

"I assumed that if my father had anything to do with it, it might be hellish. That way if it was hell, I was prepared, and if it wasn't, I was pleasantly surprised."

"That's harsh," he said. "Why do you want to go?"

"Because I have a strong feeling this may be the last time I see my father."

He decided to come along and so did my nephews who were living with me. My older nephew brought his four-year-old daughter.

By the time we met my brother at the campground he had selected, it was one hundred and four degrees. He said he chose it because he had not been there before. There was a lake, but no wading or swimming was allowed. The water glistened in the distance, tormenting us. There was also a pool, but it was closed for repairs. The campground had no trees big enough to provide any shade. It was strictly forbidden to tie anything to the only trees to create some shade, and no one was allowed to sleep on the lawn, the only bit of softness.

By Saturday evening, the campground was so crowded it was like sleeping on a freeway median. Still, my father had not shown up, and it was clear to me that he wasn't going to. But my brother did not want to leave because the campground fee was nonrefundable. I knew he was also holding hope that our father would show up.

With great effort, we talked my brother into leaving a few hours early on Sunday. Trying to redeem a bad experience, my brother suggested we go to visit a nearby ghost town. When we got there, the kids went into the Wild West Museum, and my brother and I walked around outside. When it was time for me to get the car, he said, "You should go see the little shops in that barn. I know you'll see something you like." He was right. I saw a delicate rose quartz and garnet necklace set, complete with earrings. They say rose quartz is a heart-healing stone, endowed with calming properties restoring the mind to harmony in crisis. It is said that garnets extract negativity and transmute it to a beneficial state and are used in the breastplate of the high priestess. They say it is helpful in moods of abandonment.

I thought as soon as I saw them that they were a gift for someone, but I could not figure out for whom. But I felt it so strongly that I bought them. I knew the right recipient would come to mind.

I showed the necklace and earrings to my brother and said,

"If Dad knew me, this is what he would give me." Then we parted ways.

A few miles down the road, my aunt Jane called to say, "Your father died last night. He was shot."

Everyone in the van was still and silent, waiting for my reaction. I picked up the little brown bag that held the necklace and earrings still sitting on my lap. I carefully unwrapped the earrings from their tissue paper, straightened out the wires, and laid them on the empty bag. Then, I took out the necklace and slowly balanced the tear-shaped rose quartz pendant in the very center of the dainty silver chain.

I held up the necklace and earrings where everyone could see the milky pink rose quartz and the tiny garnet glistening in the sunlight. After opening the clasp, I moved my hair out of the way, put them on thinking this is a heavenly souvenir from the vacation to hell. I said so everyone could hear, "Thanks, Dad. It is the perfect gift."

Blue Cranes Sunset Meditation

43 Part II
Light Where Darkness Had Been

By the time I arrived, my father's friends were gathering in a mob, pointing their hurt and anger at my father's girlfriend, who they thought shot him.

"We do not know what happened yet." I said.

"Clare, I know you will figure it out," my godmother said. Many throughout my life have thought I could see things others could not. When I was fourteen, my godmother saw the other kids following me around and knew I preferred solitude, so she asked sweetly, "Are your devotees crowding you, dear?"

Even as a child, people came to me thinking I had something to say that could help. I'm still trying to figure out what that is, hoping that trying is enough.

So I knew I had to show up and try to find helpful words. Hours after my father died from a shotgun blast to the head, I walked through his house trying to determine the truth I did not witness. When I opened the curtains in his bedroom where he left this earthly incarnation, I felt a rush of light fill the space where darkness had been.

Everything was perfectly neat. My father was found on his bed without a single drop of blood. His house was clean and simple with lots of books. I had a vision of my father separating himself from his own life and all his anguish. In one final courageous, though violent act, he ended his ability to do harm. In my vision, I saw him pull the trigger and lay back on the bed as if going into a final sleep.

There was no horror. I felt strongly that he was not angry, he had left nothing to be cleaned up. I felt like he was resigned to end his pain the only way he knew he could not pass it on to anyone else.

I believe he figured the family would ask me to go and find out the truth. It appeared that he did not want me to find anything disturbing. He stopped himself from hurting anyone else ever again the night before his girlfriend and her young daughter were planning to move in. I believe my father knew he could not stop himself from molesting her in any other way. I felt his final act was a selfless one. I wish he could have found another way to stop himself. I feel grateful and proud that he ended the pain instead of continuing to pass it on. I felt a certainty that it was suicide, but I wanted confirmation from outside myself.

I walked outside to consult the *I Ching: The Ancient Chinese Book of Changes*, which said, "In turning back, one is freed of guilt."

This reading confirmed what I felt and observed, that he did indeed kill himself. The police investigator came to the same conclusion. I asked the detective, "How could there be no blood?"

The detective answered, "This may be rough to hear."

"I need to know the truth, and I am okay."

"Your father knew what he was doing and was very deliberate about it. I guess he did not want you to see anything awful. He used bird shot so it would not exit his skull and closed his mouth around the barrel of the gun, so all the damage stayed inside. He sat on his bed so he would fall backward, and it left no mess."

"I really appreciate that he left me nothing horrible to find. And it is clear no one else did it because he would not have cooperated, and so there would be evidence."

"That is our conclusion as well. In a strange way, he was very considerate toward you."

"Yes, and I'm very proud he ended any possibility he would ever molest another little girl. His girlfriend and her young daughter were to be moving in today."

"You have a great attitude. That is why you are okay."

"Thanks. I am sad but okay."

I wrestled for years with sharing my story, as it is so entangled with my father's. I didn't want him to suffer despite how much pain he caused others. But as my father departed, the time to give silence a voice arrived.

After my father's suicide, I felt mostly relieved. There had always been a hard, sad place in my heart where the love of my father lived. But now my heart is soft and porous again, with no sadness sticking to it.

My father and I did not really know each other. He could not let love in, and I did not feel safe to share my truest tenderness with him. But now this feels insignificantly small, like a moth fluttering around the sun.

After the death of Kathryn, my father's firstborn, he was shaken to his core. At her memorial, my father said to me, "I have to live with what happened to you for the rest of my life," which was the first time he spoke of setting me up to be raped.

I said, "I have waited many years to hear those words. Thank you. I forgive you. Please forgive yourself." He began to weep, which I had never seen before. I held my trembling father, which was an event I did not dare hope for.

But my forgiveness was not enough, and his own forgiveness was out of reach. What he had to live with for the rest of his life, he could not tolerate. No one can know the torment anyone else has to endure. It could be that severing his brain's connection to his body was the only way to halt the dark thoughts. Maybe his guilt drove him to choose such a way to stop his anguish. Perhaps his desire to stop the violations he was compelled to commit allowed him the courage to face his fear of death. I believe that by receiving forgiveness, he did not want to have anything else to add to his self-loathing, which helped him find the strength to stop himself from hurting anyone else.

After Kathryn's memorial, he asked me to take a message to both my younger sisters apologizing for how he had hurt them. There was so much twisted stuff, and while I don't condone or excuse his hurtful behavior, I have found forgiveness, and I hope everyone can.

There is always so much to forgive in any life. I forgive them all—my father for his unhealed wounds and my older sister for taking on our father's pain and passing it on to her children. There is so much pain in the world. Many just pass on the pain passed to them, but a few courageously face the fear, hurt, and step out of the way of the anger.

While he was alive, I separated myself from the bitterness in my father's heart, keeping guard over my tenderness so his pain could not creep in. Now I can relax, as the pain my father carried and did not set down in life was resolved in death.

To my father,

I am grateful for many things you gave me: respect for nature, appreciation for keeping my mind my own, a sense of adventure, insatiable curiosity, a desire to never stop learning, creative exploration, and wit.

You showed me the dark to contrast the light, giving life more depth. I have seen you roar like a lion and tremble like a baby bird fallen from the nest. I will always remember sitting next to a fire listening to you tell stories and your passionate description of the dragons and tigers you saw in the clouds over our heads.

Most of all, I appreciate who you were and that you chose my mother. I know you did the best you could do. And in a final act I see as courage, you ended passing on the pain the only way you knew how.

Only tenderness and forgiveness remain from me for you. Now you have joined the unimaginable. I will see your magnificent creatures playing in the clouds. I will think of you when I am on an adventure.

Only love remains for you, and I hope only peace remains with you.

Your loving daughter, Clare

Protea In Glass Vase

44
Cranes On The Cliffs Of Moher In County Clare

Art is my way to find the good in everything. Creativity is how I process pain. While drawing, writing, designing, dancing, gliding, spinning, I feel free—flying without wings. Instinctively, I knew that creativity could carry me through challenges. Expression of emotion stimulates the immunological system.

When I discovered dance therapy was a profession, I felt it was a way I could be of service to the world. Catharsis, through creative movement, carried me through much adversity. The prospect of guiding others to this gift felt right.

To get a dance therapist credential, I would need a degree in dance performance before I could be an apprentice to a dance therapist. Most dancers perform for people, but I wanted to help people to dance for themselves. My inspiration is not how the dance looks, but how it feels. Not watching others express, but expressing ourselves is what offers us the most benefit. I set out to find a school where students could design their own study program. I found Antioch College in San Francisco, where I could write my own degree plan.

I fasted in solitude in the woods for three days without distractions to write my degree plan so I could find my most authentic curiosity to commit to studying. I called my degree plan, "The Study of Movement." It was all about expressing feelings through creativity for its intrinsic healing qualities.

When I shared my degree plan with my advisors, they said they did not understand it, but they trusted it. I asked them, "How can you trust it if you don't understand it?"

They said, "You understand it, and we trust you!"

"So what would you advise me to do, being you are my advisors?" They all answered a version of urging me to continue following my instincts. That made me seriously consider whether borrowing money to get a credential validating that I could educate myself made sense.

I thought it best to give it some time before deciding. I set myself up in the corner of the warehouse the school was in and did sumi-e painting exercises, wrote, played my porcelain flute, and danced.

I was curious about a class called guided imagery and music. In the class we were told to lay on the floor with our eyes closed and breathe deeply while listening to music. We each had a partner, and one of us was a guide sitting next to the one lying on the floor. In the first class, I was the guide, and my partner shared she saw her mother as a train, barreling down the tracks and running her over. She was traumatized by what she saw as were most of the students who shared their experiences.

While walking to the next class through downtown San Francisco, I passed by many struggling people who were homeless, addicted, mentally unstable, emotionally wounded, confused, and lost. With each one I passed, a weight increased on my chest. By the time I got to class, it was difficult to breathe or move. I was glad it was my turn to lay on the floor. I heard the teacher talking, but his words were without meaning to me. I couldn't think of anything but all the suffering people I passed on the way to class. I felt immense sadness. Without making any sound, I said, "Help me not turn away from the pain of others but not be crushed by it." I didn't know what or who I prayed to. I never have had certainty about this, but it does not matter. I trust the mysterious magnificence of the universe, and that is enough.

After silently asking the ineffable for help, tears rolled down my cheeks. I felt a sudden powerful shift. In the moment, I felt my cells separate, allowing more space between every molecule of my being. I could feel the music move the hair on my arms and then pass through my body. I became aware I was not solid. My body did not have a distinct edge but combined with everything surrounding it—the entire universe. I understood I was connected to and part of everything. The sounds in the room were gone, and I looked down without opening my eyes and I saw I was dancing barefoot on sharp rocks. As soon as I felt the sensation of pain on the bottom of my feet, I looked down again, and I had bird feet. Weightless on the rocks, I felt no pain. As I moved closer to the edge of the cliff, a warm wind lifted me effortlessly as I opened my large wings. Soaring along the stone edge, I did not flap; the thermals carried me. Tilting my body slightly, I flowed toward or away from the cliff's edge that dropped straight down to the ocean. Waves lapped against the stone cliff with a constant powerful rhythm.

Gliding along the rock edge, I saw a place where there was a small half-circle of stones. A few birds stood around, and one lay motionless. I descended and landed beside five birds surrounding one dead bird on a small beach made of pebbles. One of the birds asked me without a sound, "Would you like to go where birds go when they leave their bodies?"

"Yes!" was my spontaneous silent answer the birds heard. We flew upward, circling as we ascended beyond the rock cliff, rising until there was no more land or sea below and no more sky above. I could not see, hear, or feel anything but serenity and beauty.

For the first time during the class, my partner said something. "Where are you?"

"I am in the most beautiful place I've ever been!"

"What does it look like?" she asked.

"I cannot see anything," I answered.

"How do you know it is beautiful if you can't see anything?"

"It just is!" I said to her, and she didn't ask any more questions.

When we all shared our experiences, the teacher seemed to like the reports of upsetting and violent stuff the other students gave. After I spoke of my experience, he said, "You experienced false euphoria because you have not gone through the trauma to get there."

"How do you know what I have been through?" I responded. He was so upset with me, he left the class to meditate.

"I have seen this before. She is trying to take over the class," he said to the other students when he returned.

Looking at the other students, I asked, "Does anyone else think I am trying to take over the class?" No one agreed with the teacher. I left the class and realized school was not my natural way to learn. My path led elsewhere.

I dreamt the next night I was hitchhiking east on Skyline Highway, running from south of San Francisco to Santa Cruz. I consulted *The I Ching: The Ancient Chinese Book of Changes*, and it said, "It furthers one to go to the northeast corner."

So, I said my goodbyes and asked my stepsister to take me to Alice's Restaurant above Woodside, the spot from my dream. While waiting for a ride, I remembered a dream of an older woman who was dancing with the churning sea. I was so excited, thinking it was my turn to dance with the ocean, but she looked at me and pointed over to the sand dunes. I understood it was where I was to dance. Walking up the dune, I did not know what was on the other side until I got to the top and looked out at a marina full of people. Disappointed I was not to dance with the water, which felt so peaceful, I was supposed to help bring peace to the people who needed it.

On my journey, I visited Duluth. At an all-day outdoor party, nine different people told me I should teach dance. I listened, and soon after, I began my adult evening class that I called "A Way to Learn to Dance for Joy." This was only the beginning of teaching a wide range of age groups, as well as at hospitals, rehabilitation centers, and crisis shelters. I stayed for my first fall next to Lake Superior. When the birds migrated in autumn, I missed them terribly and I went to the library, assigning myself the task of drawing lines that could fly. I wanted to refine each bird to its simplest form, to do it in pen and ink with the fewest lines to portray the essence of the creature.

Years later, back in San Francisco, I realized I had to paint cranes, and I didn't question why. When I discovered the International Crane Foundation in Baraboo, Wisconsin, the one place in the world where all fifteen species lived, I decided to go. I called the director, and he invited me to visit, which I did in the winter while it was not open to the public. I was allowed to sit within the enclosures and observe the birds. While I was there, someone at a lunch gathering asked the director, "You never let me go in. How come she gets to?"

He answered in a matter-of-fact manner, "She is a crane."

When I was speaking with the administrator, she asked, "Why cranes, Clare?"

Before I could answer, she looked at me over her glasses and said, "Oh, you were one."

Those events made me recall asking my mother, "What do I say at exhibitions when people ask me why I paint birds?"

My mother answered without hesitation, "That's simple, dear. You are one."

I was keenly aware of my weight while wishing I could fly, soar, and glide. I yearned for the perspective birds have high above it all. I returned from the International Crane Foundation with six hundred pages of written information on cranes. I decided to open the pages to a random place, hoping it would help me understand my mysterious connection to the cranes. I closed my eyes and opened to the middle of the pages, putting my finger on a particular spot. Opening my eyes, I read, "The only place in all of Ireland or Scotland where the bones of cranes have been found is in County Clare and County Sligo."

Until that moment, I had not thought about what sort of bird I shape-shifted into during my experience in San Francisco many years earlier.

After my visit to the cranes, while standing in my boyfriend's kitchen, I saw a square tea can with photos of Ireland on each side. It was the first time I saw the place I flew over at eighteen years old. I walked over to the counter and picked up the tea can, and in small print at the bottom was written, "Cliffs of Moher, County Clare."

About ten years later, my dear friend Jonathan Rice, who I thought of as my spiritual father, invited me on a wild cruise along the west coast of Ireland. The Cliffs of Moher were one of the stops where we got into zodiac boats to go close to the rugged coast. As I was getting into the boat, the second officer shouted down from the pilothouse, "Tie a rope around her so she doesn't fly away."

When we got close to the rock cliff, I recognized the tiny half-circle small stone covered beach where I met the birds back in San Francisco. When we got back to the boat, a woman came up to me and said, "You must read this."

She was pointing to a particular spot in the middle of a book about the Celts. It said, "The ancient Celts, like the American Indian, could transmogrify, shape-shift, to become the

215

spirit of another creature." Reading this, I went into a soft shock and was not able to ask her why she showed this to me. I barely managed to thank her as I stumbled away in a daze.

I have no explanation for this. Trying to explain it rationally every time I am left with greater unknowns than the minuscule aspects I can comprehend. Sometimes I wonder if we carry the DNA of our human ancestors, then why would we not carry the DNA of our pre-human ancestors? Perhaps that afternoon in San Francisco, my heart was so opened by all the suffering I witnessed, I connected with my crane ancestors. Could it be we are connected to everything but only when we are wide open to notice what normally goes unnoticed? Perhaps when we are still, and our loud minds are silent, can we comprehend the natural state of the universe, where everything is interwoven. Only when we need not understand can we accept what we cannot explain.

There are rare moments when the structures we put on our lives fall away, and what remains is what is actually real. The mysterious complexity is what is authentic, and the overly simplified limitations we put on time, space, consciousness, and existence are the illusion. What I feel confident of is what we can know is insignificant compared to what we cannot. Becoming comfortable with the mystery can lead us through to amazing awareness. Thinking we can know the ineffable is an ultimate demonstration of human hubris. The only thing we can know with certainty is mysteries in this unimaginably expansive universe will continue to unfold as long as we continue to explore. I accept our unknowns will also remain elusive. I am grateful whether or not I ever know how I am connected to the cranes or the Cliffs of Moher in County Clare.

Queen Bee Ballet

45
The Dark Side Of The Moon Of Admiration

Attempting to comfort his father and my nephew about the family living in two different houses, Bodhi said, "Don't be jealous that I understand mom. It's just that I've always been in her light."

I said, "I hope this will help you to help each other heal your abandonment issues." I could no longer allow them to tag team me with their unhealed wounds, one then the other, would verbally attack me. When I tried to hold the father responsible for his actions my nephew would interrupt and defend him. When I asked my nephew a question his father would answer for him. Instead of helping each other see the negative effects of their unresolved issues, they reinforced each other's disrespectful behavior toward me. Though it was not out of cruelty but out of their fear of losing me they tried to sabotage my confidence, and in doing so, lost me. They thought controlling me made them safer. It was devastating to my happiness, health, and success. We agreed Bodhi would stay with me because he collaborated instead of competed with me.

I was so raw and empty as I left for my first vacation away from my family. I needed to find some perspective, as I had just left my sixteen-year relationship with my son's father. I left when I understood I was the only one motivated to change.

When my skating buddy's fiancé, Karma, invited me to go to a Mexican island where she had gone many times, I booked a flight to Cancun, where we would take a boat to Isla Mujeres, the Isle of Women.

As soon as we got on the island, I heard people talking about the hurricane headed for us. I asked Karma, "Did you know the hurricane was coming before we got on the airplane?"

"Yes," she said, "but I didn't want to tell you because I really wanted to go on vacation."

I said, "You didn't think I should have the information to make my own decision?"

"I didn't want to come alone."

By the time I heard anything about the storm, no boats were leaving the island because of rough seas. We booked a condo in what seemed to be the safest building on the island. It appeared even if the water washed over the island, we would be safe on the second floor of the concrete condos. I had never been in a hurricane before, and I had no idea what was coming.

Karma put her bags in her room and went to the bar with a couple of American women she knew from another trip. They returned from the bar with a bottle of tequila and continued drinking. They were all talking at the same time, none of them listening to the others. They kept taking off their clothes and cutting their skirts shorter and necklines lower and redoing their hair and makeup. I was amused for a few minutes then I started to feel compassion over how they were not comfortable with themselves no matter how many adjustments they made. They asked me to go out to the bar with them, and even though I did not want to, I thought I should socialize with these women. They may be all I have to lean on through Hurricane Isidore.

They took us to a bar with loud salsa playing on a jukebox. There was a tall Austrian man who owned property on the island, and they seemed to know him well. He bought all their tequila shots. I was amazed at how many they could drink and still function. He offered to buy me drinks, but I declined. I had no interest in getting intoxicated. I had not been in a hurricane and felt I needed my wits about me.

A young man came into the bar, and Karma danced very close to him. He asked me to dance, and I love all dancing, especially salsa, so I said yes. "You are what I have been waiting for," he whispered while we danced. I could tell Karma had some relationship with him, and I did not want him to have any misunderstanding.

I simply said, "No, you have not been waiting for me! Thanks for the dance." I left the dance floor and decided to say goodnight and walk back to the condo.

The next day, Karma and her two friends showed up hungover and grumpy and started snorting cocaine. When they offered me some, I said, "No thanks! I have a terrible reaction to drugs."

After they got high, they started saying things like, "You are the goddess, the spiritual teacher, the wise one. You are so beautiful. You should let the doctor take pictures of you at the goddess temple."

I responded, "We are all beautiful. We should take pictures of each other, not have a man do it."

I heard a voice inside say, "They are not who they represent themselves to be." Having had no rest, the pressure of the hurricane approaching, and my vulnerability having just left a sixteen-year relationship, I was not thinking clearly. So when they invited their male friend over, I talked to him in the living room while they were getting louder in the kitchen. The wind started to blow hard, but they decided to go out drinking again, and he stayed behind.

After they left, I talked to him, hoping to enlist his assistance in what I felt was approaching. I was nervous about the hurricane, but what I feared most was the women turning on me. It did not occur to me he would be part of it.

He said, "They admire you."

"Perhaps," I replied, "but jealousy is the dark side of the moon of admiration, and it can turn in an instant."

My instincts took over when I saw the look in his eyes I had not seen since I had been raped as a teenager. He lunged at me, and without hesitation, I rolled off the couch before he could get on top of me with his muscled body. I stood up in a flash and immediately backed away. He jumped up. I backed out onto the balcony, and he followed me.

I said, "You were different last night. You were a gentleman. What happened to you?"

"They gave me cocaine." As he followed me out on the balcony, I looked down and saw the sand dune as my way out. I jumped, rolled, and ran.

The hurricane's driving rain and wind strength were more powerful than I had ever experienced. I found a hall under a staircase where I hid for hours, trying to imagine how to survive all of it. I could not get off the island or even make a phone call. I did not know anyone but him, Karma, and her altered friends. It became clear I had to protect myself, and I was committed to doing so. I returned to my condo and entered silently, leaving the door open in case he was still there. When I was sure no one was there, I locked the front door and put a pan that would move loudly if the door was opened. I brought fresh water, food, a candle, matches, a knife, and a broken broom handle into my room. I put the knife under my mattress on one side of my bed and the broken broom handle on the other side and practiced getting them quickly in the dark. I put a chair under my doorknob.

I cleared the path to my window so I could jump out onto the sand dune if I needed an escape route again. I lit a candle instead of turning on the light so no one could see I was there. Finally, I felt safe enough to cry and let written words be my sacred witness:

When Hurricane Isadore
Came to Isla Mujeres
Palms quivered and bowed
Even the sea followed his lead
Nothing could resist the fierce beauty
The winds roared when he roared
The rains poured when he poured
All followed his every movement
In his presence the trees on the Isle of Women
Exposed their roots to the stars
Sky rivers flowed on land
No one was unmoved
Nothing was untouched
Every speck of sand under the gigantic sky
Undulating seas surge and submit
Everyone came seeking sustenance
From the inexhaustible well
Hoping hearts were swept along
In the destructive dance
For those who came to take
Could not enter the inner sanctum
Those who came to give were embraced
Filled with his grace
Everything was suspended
In the whirling trance of Isidore's dance.

I watched Hurricane Isidore bend the palm trees until they were parallel with the ground. I wrote by candlelight watching the storm roar outside while listening to hear any sounds inside. I fell into sleep a few times over the night and felt great relief when the sun rose. No one came in through the night. Now with the sunlight, I thought I could deal with whatever I had to.

Even the strengthening winds were not as scary in the light. I watched the angle of the leaning palm trees to judge the strength of the storm as it increased for the next few days. I stayed in the condo, conserving my energy. As I wrote and was still and quiet, I felt increasingly confident.

Karma came a few times during the next couple of days to get some clothes. She barely spoke to me. I stayed distant and only said hello and goodbye.

On the ninth day on the island, I had been alone for days when Karma and her two friends showed up. They were all animated and jerky. They seemed even louder and more graceless. Perhaps it was all my solitude and quiet, or maybe they had been drinking and doing drugs nonstop.

One of them asked me why I didn't want to go out with them. I said, "I felt like being alone after your friend tried to jump me the night you left him here."

"Well, you need a good fucking," the blonde one said.

"Wow," I said.

Then Karma said, "Yeah you're too attached to dignity."

Outraged, I said, "I'm not attached to dignity; I am dignity. And you guys used to be too. We are all born dignified. What happened to your dignity? Maybe you misplaced your dignity, but it's not too late to find it. Perhaps you should look for it before it is."

The blonde said, "You think you're better than us."

"No, I don't think I'm better than you or anyone else. But I do think I act better sometimes, like now, for instance."

They were stunned for a moment before the blonde said, "We told him you are the kind of woman he had to take." At that moment, I thought the women must have been getting the cocaine from the doctor, which was why they wanted me to pose for him at the temple on the island, instead of taking photos of each other. The time I went out with them I saw that they were getting the tequila from the Austrian man, and then I figured out they tried to set me up as payment for their bad habits. I was so disheartened by all of it, and tears came to my eyes. I felt the need to get away from them in the dining room, and I went into the living room and sat down to compose myself.

The blonde came over to me and yelled, "You need to get fucked to get you off your high horse." She was so angry when she spoke, she was spitting in my face, "You're the kind of woman he would marry, and I was fucking him up until you got here."

All of a sudden, I heard my departed mother's voice as if she was right next to me. "Stand up, dear!" It was then that I realized I was in great danger, and I stood up and opened my mouth not knowing what was going to come out. I just knew I had to get away from them before they hurt me, which I now understood was what they wanted. I instantly imagined a backup plan where I would pick up the lamp in front of me and hit the blonde first if she struck me and then Karma and the other one if they tried to stop me from leaving.

Confident I could defend myself against all three of them, I pointed at the door and said with a certainty and force shocking even me, "That is the door. I am going out, and if you try to stop me, you will see a ferocity you didn't know existed on this planet!"

They all froze and held their breath as I walked out of the condo. I kept picking up my pace down the hall and stairs. When I was outside, I ran out to the beach, and I continued running for a mile. I didn't realize the hurricane had passed until I stopped and fell to my knees, and the first light came through the clouds. I started laughing, remembering what I said. I laughed for a long time.

I went back to pack in the middle of the night and took my bag to the beach cafe next to the condo as I waited for the sun to come up. The waiter brought me coffee and sat next to me. I realized he must have heard all of it through the open windows. He said, "You live in the light. You will be fine. You are admirable." I realized he was right. I would be fine. But I knew they would not be fine because they lived on the dark side of the moon of admiration.

Storm Over Grand Canyon

46
Off The Mountain Of Silence
Flows A River Of Words

When my mother came to live with me as an adult, I asked her, "What was your greatest worry about me when I was a child?"

She answered without hesitation, "That you would find a sanctuary on a mountaintop, and we would never see you again." Instead, I try to create sanctuary and invite the trustworthy in. I have always craved solitude while pondering what makes people happy. In my contemplative time, I am always thinking about others. I believe my best contribution is the creativity that comes from caring about everyone—all life forms and the environment in my solitude. Art is my way to reconcile these two potentially opposing impulses. I do my work alone in preparation to give it to the world. While apart from others, I think, draw, and write, pondering what makes people happy.

Years of prose in front of me, I wonder if I would have survived without these pages as my sacred witness. Pages and pages of healing words. So many things I needed to say but did not dare speak them out loud. Some of these truths so desperately needed to be expressed but were too dangerous to be shared. These sacred witness pages, keepers of my secrets, saving me from the quiet, keeping my heart from going silent.

Now I have come to understand it is more courageous to share my quiet place than to stay inside of it. Staring at these blank, icy white pages is like looking down the steep, snow-covered mountain the first time I skied, knowing as soon as I crept over the edge, gravity would be in charge. There will be no turning back. I've made my choice between staying safe on top of the mountain of silence or hurling myself down into the avalanche of articulations. Stillness is melting and flowing off the mountain of silence as a river of words.

I have given myself no escape. Taking a huge breath, I hear a silent voice say, "All you have to do is begin," and so I do. Here I go!

I am witnessing my own story unfolding as I follow this adventure into knowing my own unknown. After years of waiting to set my story free, I let the words speak to me as I speak them. I have feared I will be consumed by the pain of the truth. A voice within says, "The truth will not hurt you, but secrets will."

I have no answers, only questions. What do I have to say? What value could my words have for anyone else? All I know is I have a heart ready to open to the world and trust it is enough.

My pencil is laying next to pages I have been writing since I was fourteen. Some of these words hurt with the original intensity years later as I read them. Others were so vulnerable that they needed to be written in code. As an infant's utterances make no sense to adults, but are still true, some words stay safe by being obscure, like a lullaby in another language cannot be understood but still soothes.

Let the words speak to me and set my story free. Through the eyes of others, perhaps I can get a more complete view of myself.

Words most needing to be spoken can take the longest to surface. For years after I was raped, I was filled with silent shame. I felt as if I was somewhat responsible. Somehow I brought it on myself. I did not realize the self-blame did not come from inside but from outside. It came from society not accepting its own sickness. Many people are terrified by violence, so they cannot admit perfectly innocent people are violated. Many cannot fathom we cannot protect ourselves or our loved ones from all harm. Sometimes those who did nothing to deserve it and could not have done anything to prevent it can be victims anyway. There are those who cannot bear to live in an unfair and unkind world, so they make up a reality they can live with, where the victim could have prevented the assault. I am no longer angry at them for their misunderstanding or fear blaming the victim. I forgive them their confusion. It was once my own.

I hid my pain. I was ashamed it happened to me. I thought anyone who knew would fear me or think of me as broken. It used to hurt, but now I know fear makes us myopic.

226

Only love expands our perspective. I understand why people want to believe we get what we deserve. We do not want to believe life can be random. We do not want to accept innocent people can suffer great injustice. We want to think we have control over what happens to us.

But, I believe we can take comfort in knowing there is a sort of justice in the universe. Ultimate justice is we all have to live with ourselves and what we do. Everyone pays for their acts by not being able to hide from their own truth. It will haunt us in our dreams or poison our well of self-love. No one can escape themselves.

Those who are cruel find no peace. Regrets offer no mercy, and the judgment we cannot escape is our own. To feel peace, we must face ourselves and accept everything that has been done to us and what we have done to others. It is difficult to accept having been raped, but I have found peace with it and myself, which I doubt ever truly happens for the rapist.

How many times in life I have felt pain, shame, rage, forgiveness, and acceptance. How many years it took me to forgive myself for the violence done to me. How strongly, as a young person, I believed what others believed and thought less of myself for someone else's inhumanity. I did what society wants victims to do—loathed myself and kept my shame silent. No more! Telling the truth can be painful, but it is how we heal. Being honest is how we evolve beyond surviving into thriving.

I want to give my story to the world to connect the open hearts and help open closed ones. The story is not important, but a willingness to tell it is. I tell my story to set it down and walk away, clearing space for all the other stories yet to be. I do not say it because I want to repeat it, but because I don't want to repeat it. By giving my story away, it has no more power over me. I tell it to get to the silence underneath—the calm eye in the center of the storm of words. There is a stillness beyond the story—a pure place where truth lives.

The admirable thing about writing is not what we write but our willingness to be alone long enough to write it. It is so easy to distract ourselves endlessly with one activity then the next. But to be still enough to find our truth, to feel our feelings, to think our thoughts, to discover our guiding principles, is remarkable.

Interesting stories often contain difficulty, but that is not what makes them interesting. It is how the difficulties are resolved that make them inspirational. How we heal from assault is fascinating; assault is not. Healing comes from sharing without shame the shameful things that happen to us. We are not free of it until we also accept that while we are not responsible for what is done to us, we are responsible for healing it.

We all have to deal with pain. If we have not been assaulted, someone we love has. Everyone has to deal with it. We are all connected. When any of us is wounded, we are all hurt.

My story is not interesting because I've been assaulted but because I have not forsaken love. Any of us continuing to love against all odds is the greatness of being human.

My mother loved, understood, and forgave everyone all the time for everything. She did not hold grudges. The only times I saw her angry were in defense of me. Then, like a mother bear, her righteous indignation was fierce.

My father passed his unhealed wounds on to others. I am embracing the duality of life—fear making us myopic and love expanding us. Trusting words can help others, making all we go through inconsequential in comparison. Let pour my river of words off the mountain of silence.

Dolphins Golden Gate Bridge Space

47
Destiny's Mixing Bowl

Here the place of my birth, I see my story not as my story, but our story. We are all stirred together here in a mixing bowl of destiny. Today, layers of mystery fall away like spent cactus blossoms after giving away their beauty. I am filled with this place and with the recognition I have been blessed by every one of the ten thousand turns of my life, finding its way back to where it began. I am filled with gratitude for this place.

What is it about this place that drew us in? Why was my spark of life kindled here? Why, years later, did the man who raped me flee to this place that night when his act transformed me from child to woman in a minute? Why, years later, did my father return here to end his own life?

Now I am returning to this place for my godmother's memorial service, and I am wondering what it is about this place for me. Is it the mountain ranges circling it like a gigantic bowl, stirring powerful spirits together? Could it be the magnetism of the circle of mountains surrounding it? Is it the peaks creating a vortex drawing in my unborn spirit? Was I lured here by the invisible swirling energy?

Here everything is enormous. Even the emptiness is gigantic. The space in between things is immense. The expanse is the desert's soul. The void is the desert's heart. Everything is bigger: crime, churches, immense disappointments, and enormous hearts.

Boundaries disappear here in the desert, and the sky blends with the sand. The wide-open desert sky dissolves any illusion we are separate—all of our differences evaporate.

It is an intersection between the north and south, heaven and hell, saints and sinners, thorns and blooms. The cosmos is always watching here. Everyone is exposed to the power of the undiluted elements. The tremendous energy here drags some down and propels some up. It has one of the highest crime rates in the nation, giving the good people plenty to do.

My godmother went out with my father before my mother did. What if they became my parents? My godfather went out with my mother before my father did. What if they were my parents? How would I be different? Would I be any of me? Would I have the same spirit but a different bone structure? Would I be an entirely different person? Maybe half of me, but which half?

My godmother was saintly like my mother, but a flamboyant saint, while my mother was a shy one. Both qualified as enlightened beings in my eyes because they both lived lives full of kindness and compassion. They were selfless examples of excellent humanness. My godmother worked within the church and my mother outside of it. They honored each other's differences and remained dear friends throughout their lives.

My godfather and father were as different as my mother and godmother were similar. My godfather was quiet, straightforward, and deliberate in speech and actions. My father was loud, complicated, and explosive. My godfather trusted his inner worth and faith. My father tried to prove his worth and intelligence. Somehow, their fundamental differences did not ever interfere with their friendship, which survived their lifetimes.

As I fly over this place, houses below me are as tiny as matchbooks. Even the tracks of homes look tiny. All my earthly concerns have become minuscule. I watch the river below curve in one thousand graceful turns.

When I told my six-year-old son Bodhi I was going to my godmother's funeral, he reached deep inside and said, "She has gone to be with God. That is what godmothers do!" He continued, "Some people just have too much life!"

She did have too much life. She was always active. If she was not doing something for one of her six children, seven grandchildren, or many godchildren, she was doing something for someone less fortunate than herself, and there was always someone less fortunate than her.

My godmother lived within what she believed to be true without ever imposing it on others. Her unwavering conviction, unconditional acceptance, and spiritual practice was an inspiration to me. Her loving assistance to others was constant, selfless, and authentic. She was driving the Holy Eucharist to the

231

homebound when she was killed instantly when her van was hit by a truck at an intersection. The priest said this gave her an express route to heaven. Her course was laid long ago—a direct route to the divine.

Now, family and friends move like a swarm of bees following the flower from the mortuary to the church and finally to the mausoleum. Love floods the space in between all concerns and fears. I can see so much more beauty. I feel a stronger connection to the indescribable.

I say goodbye to you without regret that you have gone back to the ineffable. As Bodhi said, "That is what godmothers do." I have been gifted to know you. Your compassion is always with me. Thank you for seeing me and encouraging me to dream.

Thank you for all the times I came to you exhausted, for you to ask, "Are your devotees crowding you, dear?" You taught me how to find my own space in between. Your love without conditions still gives me courage. Thank you for taking me in when I had colic and my mother had two other toddlers. Thank you for telling me that when my colic lifted, I became content, and all I needed was a little kiss every once in a while. It is true that imagining your kiss when I need it, every once in a while, gets me through. I feel destiny's mixing bowl will always be stirring us together.

Demoiselle Cranes In Winter

48
Passing Through Walls

The dawn has a stillness, infusing the sky, mountains, and air with otherworldliness. The rarity of the sparkling white on the mountaintops melts as the wind blows. The shining dust is magical this morning. Everything is glowing from the inside. The red, orange, yellow, green, blue, indigo, and violet arches over the valley. It is soon followed by hail. It is exhilarating and frightening. The mountain looks like a landscape painted with royal foliage and a perfectly blue sky. The beauty is intoxicating. I imagine dancers sprinkling snow on the peaks. Flurries rise up and circle in graceful turns. I sense fantastic power all around. I become aware of how small I am. Everything about this day is wild and beautiful and suggests I should predict the unpredictable.

I call Glenda and say, "This is the sort of day where anything could happen. I feel it would be good for me to come off the mountain I live on and go out tonight and dance and celebrate life."

It is the best night out dancing I have ever had. My understanding of human nature takes a leap forward when I try something unusual on this special day. I invite the lusty men hovering on the periphery and the insecure women watching from the walls to dance, instead of avoiding them all. I dance with them all at once, and then I dance away from them and let them dance with each other. They stop projecting hostility, and the lusty, jealous, competitive, and aggressive energy transforms into playful joy. I invite the dark into the light, and everyone has fun. No one feels left out, and I feel safe.

While driving Glenda home after hours of blissful dancing and drinking only water, I feel great. I feel sure I should give her a driving lesson on what to do if you go into a skid because she is learning to drive. I begin by demonstrating pulling my feet back from the pedals so they cannot react and hit the brake and cause the vehicle to spin.

I tell her, "Do nothing sudden. Do not hit the brakes. No jerking the steering wheel. Turn gently into the spin. Don't panic. Move smoothly and do everything softly. Keep breathing, keep thinking, dance gracefully through it, stay light, don't give in to fear, and it will all be okay."

I am feeling it as I say it, "It is like being on skates. You have to float and gently maneuver because you have no brakes when you are sliding on ice. We have to go with it and ever so softly. Do the best you can do until you have traction again to avoid hitting anything." I rehearse the moves like a dancer practices the choreography before a performance. I wonder if I am terrifying her because of how real I am making it. But I think she needs to know what a dangerous dance it can be. I need her to understand that lives are at stake.

After dropping her off, I head toward my mountain home in light rain. I drive across the Golden Gate Bridge. I enter the tunnel above Sausalito, tired but happy. Halfway through the tunnel, I see a wall of white just outside the end of the tunnel, and I recognize it immediately. I move over one lane to the right and slow down as much as I can without letting any of the cars behind me crash into me. I can tell the cars behind me are unaware of what is awaiting us just outside the tunnel. We are all about to exit the tunnel into another world. The freak blizzard drops six inches of snow on top of black ice in fifteen minutes. As soon as I leave the tunnel, I sense death is close by. I pull my feet back just as I demonstrated to Glenda. Cars are going sideways and backwards into the guardrail and the center concrete barrier. I feel the terror we all feel and I know I have to focus on my breath and not let fear take over.

Immediately I start chanting, "Keep breathing, keep choosing to protect all life. Keep breathing, keep choosing to protect all life." I keep saying it over and over, and it keeps me calm as I slip and slide.

Then I remember what I said to Glenda less than an hour before I needed to hear it. As I pass vehicles spinning, sliding backwards, skidding sideways, rebounding off the median, I start feeling terror rising in my body, and I start chanting again, "Keep breathing, keep choosing to protect all life." I focus on hitting

235

nothing, floating, gliding, skidding, and choosing a path through the chaos.

As I climb an incline, my speed slightly decreases as does the number of vehicles making it this far before spinning out of control or hitting something to stop them. I begin to feel hopeful I will reach pavement and regain my ability to steer.

I reach the summit of the hill and begin to pick up speed as I descend. My van is hydroplaning, skimming the water's surface on top of the ice, with virtually no friction. No one can slow down. I am the only one periodically able to steer. Everyone else is sliding out of control.

Having no way to slow my vehicle down, it gets harder not to panic, and I chant louder, "Keep breathing, keep choosing to protect all life." Then I see my long-departed mother out in front of me in the blizzard. She is made out of a cloud and is reaching her long delicate fingers down to the icy freeway and gently sweeping a path for the spinning and sliding vehicles not to hit each other and clearing a safe passage for me. My feeling of panic turns to trust in inexplicable forces. I have just enough turning ability to take the safe path through the wreckage and chaos by making minor adjustments, and I continue past crashed vehicles, one after another.

Everything is moving in slow motion as I am going downhill on the ice. My speed is still increasing. I see a wall of stopped cars spanning the entire freeway ahead. I have no way to slow down or go around the mangled vehicles. There is no way not to crash into the wall of twisted vehicles. The best I can do is choose the place I will hit metal where there won't be people behind doors. I pick a spot where two cars are facing each other with their front bumpers touching. I have so much time to think about death, and I have a thought, it would be ironic if, after the best night of dancing in my life, it is my last. I also think accidents are often started by intoxicated people who sometimes are too drunk to be afraid and can come out okay, and sober people like myself can end up hurt or killed because they tense up in fear. I decide to have a happy thought before I hit the wall. I do not want to be afraid or angry if it is my time. Grateful somehow, I have the presence of mind and just enough steering not to crash into a door. If I have to go, I do not want to take anyone else with

236

me. This thought makes me happy. It occurs to me that I did not tell Glenda what you do if you have no options—let go!

I imagine myself as a big rag doll in a bumper car game just before I gently steer toward the two front bumpers and turn my right front bumper to hit first. I close my eyes, go limp, and let go of the steering wheel.

I recall a vision I had years before while fasting when I asked the ineffable how can I survive, and a voice said, "Be the warrior rag doll." Just before impact, I am going almost sixty miles an hour, and I know it could be my last thought, and I choose to feel grateful. I have almost finished the website of my art, and I trust my son will get it out to the world if I cannot. I become the warrior rag doll who cannot be harmed by anyone who does not love her and will not be harmed by those who do.

I hit the bumpers, and they part. I pass through, and the two vehicles behind me pass through the opening I created and hit me, one after another. I smell what I think is fire but is propellant from the airbag. The front of my van is so torn apart, the metal carves into the ice, and it comes to a stop on the incline. I open my eyes and jump out of my van without turning off the engine. I get off the freeway and away from the path of the next vehicle to hit. As the next car crashes into the wall of stopped cars, the other people standing by the road scream. I do not scream, feeling I need to conserve my energy to get through this and help others. Once the terrible metal hitting metal sounds stop, I go to my van and get the thirty coats I have behind my van's back seat. I think about my son saying, "Why do you have so many jackets in your van?"

"Because you never know." Every time someone came up the mountain and left their coat, I would put it in my van. Now, an utterly unpredictable blizzard hits where no one has ever seen one before. Here I am with just enough jackets for all the women in skimpy outfits in shock in a snowstorm. Life can be perfect, even in its most painful moments. Adversity shows us the enormous resources within. The wall of metal was a mysterious portal, reminding me just how precious life is. I am committed to turning everything to the good, especially the difficult, by learning from it. Watch over everyone. Give whatever you can, whether it is a coat, a calming word, a silent presence, or a reassuring touch. Most importantly, give to the givers.

Mysteriously, I was prepared and guided through it and in a position to help others. It was an ordeal I am better for having gone through. Do not fear but accept the unexpected could be just ahead. If a difficulty arises, keep breathing, keep choosing to protect all life, not just our own, and do not give up! If the unavoidable is in our path, no matter how hard, we must let go just before impact.

Two women died in the pileup. One died before I got there, and the second woman died in the arms of a young doctor who was also involved in the pileup. He came away from the group and was standing close to me when he called his mother. He wept, saying, "I couldn't help her. I did everything I was trained to do, but I couldn't help her."

The incident manager arrived at the scene and was overwhelmed, pacing back and forth next to my van, away from all the ambulances, fire trucks, and police cars. I put on one of my jackets and walked next to him, saying, "None of us is prepared for this. There is no precedence, so there was no training, but we will figure it out together. I have jackets for every woman so that no one will get hypothermic." He turned and looked at me with a grateful but puzzled expression and then walked over to face the horror and do his job.

The emergency responders didn't even have space blankets to give those who were not wearing enough clothes and had been drinking and were in shock. I walked around the outside of the group gathered in one place to assess who needed the jackets I had. I walked up behind the shivering women and put the coats over their shoulders. Each of them turned and looked at me surprised, like I was an angel. Some nodded, some gave a tiny smile, a few whispered thank you, but most were too cold to speak.

Those of us who were not injured were taken to the police station. I was taken in the last group many hours later just before it got light. When I arrived, I noticed an exhausted priest who had been talking to people for hours. He came over to me, looking distraught and exhausted. He asked, "How come you're not crying like everyone else?"

238

I answered, "Because they need our help. I will cry later."

He gave a sweet little grin and said, "I needed that."

Then I saw a fireman I recognized whimpering in the corner. I walked over to him and said, "You saved my son's life."

"There were no children in the pileup," he said.

"A few years ago, when my 14-year-old son and his friends tried liquor for the first time, my son was taken to the hospital. The police were not going to let me leave to be with him until you stepped up and took responsibility for the other boys. He had the highest blood alcohol the hospital emergency room had ever seen. He did not die, and I believe it was because I was there touching him and talking to him. Otherwise, he would have just slipped away. You saved his life. We cannot save everybody, but we can save some if we keep trying." He looked at me with sweet gratitude and came out of his despair about not being able to save either of the two women who died in the pileup.

As I was leaving, I saw the young doctor who called his mother next to my van while we were all waiting for the ambulances, and I said, "You did help her."

He got angry and snapped back at me, "But she died."

"Yes, she did die, but she died in the arms of a kind stranger who risked his own safety to try to help her. She died feeling cared for. You did help her."

His face softened as his anger turned to acceptance. He did what he could. He took a deep breath and said, "Thank you."

I cried for hours once home, recalling every moment of the dangerous dance, slipping and sliding and somehow passing through a wall of stopped cars at almost sixty miles an hour unharmed. Then I remembered being a very young child and asking the divine to let me pass through the wall. I would bump into the wall over and over until I stopped asking for proof of the existence of the ineffable. Now I wondered if I could have known at some point I would need to pass through the wall. I laughed thinking about me as a little girl trying to get the divine to demonstrate its power on command. Did some benevolence in the universe grant my request, not when I wanted it, but when I needed it? I'm comfortable with not knowing. Gratitude that I did pass through the wall is enough.

Napa Valley Three Palms Vineyard

49

The Crafty Christian And The Honest Atheist

A tropical island can be a place to repair and replenish. But at any watering hole, predators can be waiting. They are waiting to see the light of innocence leaking out of the holes abuse puts in the heart.

We should not judge people by what they believe, but how they behave. Those who seek out the vulnerable by seeing their wounds are especially dangerous and vile.

When our son was old enough to be okay without me for a while, I went to a tropical island. I needed to gain perspective from a man whose wounds did not become visible until after I was carrying his child. For years, I put my compassion for him and my hope the family could stay together above my happiness.

Through my unconditional loving support, he quit cocaine, alcohol, womanizing, and not working. He got clean and became prosperous, but I paid the price. I became his everything: mother of his child, counselor, business consultant, estate manager, secretary, sweetheart, and best friend. He became utterly dependent on me while his fear of losing me caused him to try to control me, by any means necessary. I had to get away, and when I returned, he yelled at me, saying, he did not exist without me. And I accepted I had to individuate without telegraphing my plan to do so, or I could be a casualty.

I needed to restore by being alone in nature. I went to the rainbow trees, jungle waterfalls, bamboo groves, lavender farms, walked in tropical air, swam in a warm ocean, and watched a mother whale with her young.

The only people I knew on the island had left on a European vacation, and I was feeling very alone. A man who had long lived on the island offered to be my tour guide. I told him I had no interest in romance, he said that was fine because he had a girlfriend. I felt safe to go sightseeing with him because I would be driving, and just in case, I had a taser my son gave me for Mother's Day.

Before we got to the bamboo forest, I was irritated by Valentine talking about himself as a healing Christian. Keeping distance from him, I heard him say the same lines to everyone. As we walked, I was embarrassed for him and did not want anyone to think I was with him. It astounded me how many gave him their contact information simply because he had a seemingly innocent smile. He had perfected his lines that temporarily took me in. It amazed me what a big, pushy white guy saying, "Bless you. God loves you," could convince others of. His technique was to just keep talking until they turned over their information. He got a lot of phone numbers. Perhaps some gave him a phony number, while others maybe thought it was the quickest way to get rid of him and would not answer when he called, but some went for it, as I did for a few minutes.

He said to me, "We make a good team," and I knew I had to get away from him at the first opportunity. I didn't feel right leaving him in the bamboo forest just because I thought he was obnoxious.

So I said, "I am hungry." He directed us to a restaurant I found out later was the most expensive on the island.

He ordered the most costly dinner on the menu and then faked surprise as he said, "Oh, darn. I forgot my wallet."

As he worked everyone around us, I said, "I'm going outside to take some pictures." I grabbed the check without him seeing, and I gave the hostess enough cash for our dinners and a tip, walking as fast as I could without running to the valet. "I have to go right now!" The valet seemed to understand and ran to my car. He hopped out, throwing open the driver's door in one smooth movement. I jumped in, tossing him a tip as I raced out of the parking lot. I felt enormous relief to be out of the crafty Christian's presence. Imagining him standing in the parking lot and wondering what happened made me laugh a little, thinking about how the self-proclaimed seer didn't see that coming.

I made sure he did not know where I was staying. I left him one message saying, "You are not a healing artist, as you say you are; you are a con artist. Do not call me ever again."

Unfortunately he got the phone number where I was staying because I left one message when I thought he would respect my wishes and not contact me anymore. But I was wrong.

I did not answer any of his increasingly frantic phone messages. With every message, his desperation and anger increased. He called over and over, leaving messages so long the machine cut him off before he stopped talking. His messages eventually filled the tape, and the phone rang twenty times in a row before he gave up. I erased all his messages off my friend's answering machine in case someone else wanted to leave a message. The phone started ringing again, and the answering machine took another urgent message. This one said, "Call me because I have been getting things coming through I need to share with you. Your ancestors are giving me information to give you." I think if my ancestors have information for me, they will tell me! I recall him saying to everyone, "I am a healer." I thought, then heal yourself. Then he tried demanding I answer. It felt good to hit delete after each of his increasingly hostile messages. I remember he put some clothes in my car as if our sightseeing excursion was going to turn into spending days together. Perhaps his girlfriend threw him out. Regardless, I didn't want the bad karma of throwing his stuff away.

There was no way I wanted to see him again, so I looked for a police station to leave his things at. I found a local fire station and rang the bell, but no one answered. Remembering there was an honest-looking older man with his dog in front of his stove store, I went there and asked, "Where is the police station?"

"There isn't one," he said, stroking the old dog's shoulder.

"Explains why I couldn't find it," I replied.

"What do you need?"

"I went sightseeing with a man who is not who he represented himself to be, so I took off. I asked him to not contact me, and he won't stop calling. He left some stuff in my car I want to get rid of."

"I'll handle it," he said. "Just give me his number, and I'll tell him to come get his shit!"

I handed the store owner the phone number and the grifter's stuff. I held out a twenty, saying, "For your trouble."

"I don't want any money, and I don't want to know your name," he said with a sweet firmness.

"I knew you were a gentleman when I passed you and your dog the other day. When you call him he's going to try to run his shifty spiritual speak on you."

"Won't work on me. I'm an atheist."

I laughed, thinking about the honest atheist telling the crafty Christian, "Come get your shit!"

"Thank you again," I said, shaking his hand. Soon after, the crafty Christian's phone calls stopped. When my friends returned, I told them the story, and they said, "Somehow, the worst guy on the island found you, and you found the best guy on the island to deal with him."

Once home, after getting perspective, I saw clearly I had to get away from him without letting him know when or where I was going. Now I understand people sometimes feel they must destroy who they cannot control. I do want to love everyone, some up close, some at arm's length, and some from a distance. Only those whose actions and words are aligned should be trusted like the honest atheist. I do not want to hate anyone, like the crafty Christian.

Avocado Seed In Space

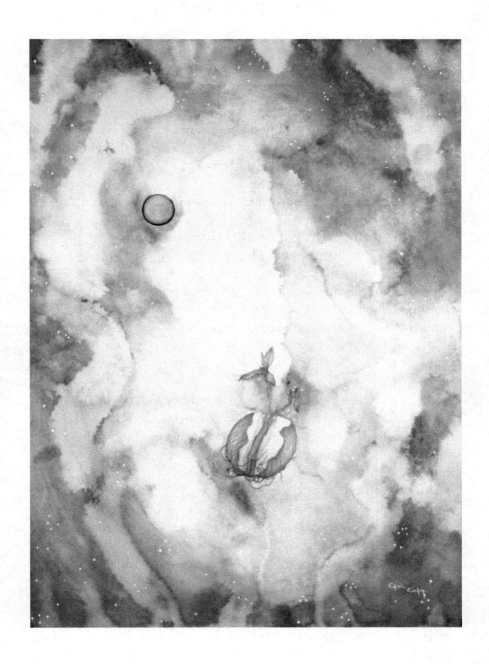

50
Sanctuary Under Siege

Struggles of epic proportions can happen when our wounds get entangled. Some of our unresolved issues can complement each other. Our missing parts can appear to match up perfectly as they whirl around each other in a dizzying dance of dysfunction. We can misunderstand it as wholeness and together feel complete, for a while.

An artist and an attorney, one feeling, the other analyzing. One trying to observe the truth, the other trying to convince others of their truth. The artist's nature attempts to see the natural order in the cosmos. The attorney's instincts are to create unnatural order using laws.

An empathic person can attract those lacking empathy, as material acquisition can dazzle those without it. My lack of exposure to finances misunderstood his economic development as a sort of balance between us. My spiritual development made him feel safe, as he said I was the person he most trusted with his life.

Opposites can attract, but sometimes they attract trouble. We all have different skills and perspectives, which can be beautifully functional when we combine our differences, collaborate not compete, which I hoped for, until I could no longer.

The message I carried from my dysfunctional upbringing said, take care of everyone, or no one will survive. He told me his message from his early abandonment was, don't share, and take care of yourself because no one else will. We did what had become natural. I tried to care for everybody, while he tried to control everybody. We both still follow our prime directive, but I have finally put myself at the top of the care for everyone list.

Being selfless was actually selfish because it allowed my inner resources to be used up by a few, so I could not give to all those I could give to if I was not drained. Being selfish enough to protect my joy is truly selfless because now I have the space to do my work that may help many. When I realized this, I said, "You cannot share me with the world, so you have to give me to the world."

Those who do not see harmonious relationships growing up may not recognize the signs of being in an unhealthy one. I did not see any of this before I got pregnant. While I was pregnant, it felt like he changed from treating me like a partner to a possession. I spoke of this in therapy with him many times. He always appeared to care and said what I wanted to hear, but he did not change which caused me sadness. Wanting so badly for us all to remain a family, I stayed loyal, patient, and supportive, hoping he would learn to collaborate instead of compete with me.

Staying busy caring for the family was automatic. Keeping productive doing my art, creativity retreats, exhibitions, readings, performances, hosting friends' weddings, memorial services, lectures and workshops with the Institute of Noetic Sciences; Freedom to Roam, Patagonia's nonprofit wing; and the Fetzer Institute kept my focus on giving to others.

Inviting a Japanese master woodworker, an Austrian filmmaker, a Mexican-American and her daughter, a male German high school exchange student, and an Ethiopian woman who became part of the family to live with us over the years exposed my family to many cultures and nationalities and distracted me from my discontent.

After years of repeating, "I need to be heard to be happy," I became spiritually allergic to not being heard. Then, when my father figure took me on a trip away for the first time, my natural enthusiasm returned until I came home and accepted that my son's father had no motivation to change because I took care of him and his feelings. I realized I had to change, and I went on a silent retreat. He went on a number of trips every year, but his reaction to me claiming some time for myself was so negative I decided to be celibate for a year as final notice for him to change. I wanted to keep the family together, so I moved into the sauna room and no longer shared a bed with him. I waited until our son was thirteen, thinking he was old enough to be okay, and I told him I had left his father years earlier.

Some say those who feel a lot are too sensitive, but no one ever says they wish the world had more insensitive people in it. It is easy not to feel. It takes courage to feel deeply. Coming from hurt is effortless; coming from compassion takes effort. I committed young to treat everyone with respect because it is what everyone, including me, wants. Treating each other respectfully makes life, relationships, communities, and the world better. Hearing each other is part of being respectful. In family therapy, I defined respect as trying to hear the other and show concern for their feelings. Disrespect defends, denies, dismisses, diminishes, or denigrates. If those close to us do not try to hear us and show concern for our feelings, it is our duty to move to a safe distance to protect our tenderness instead of forfeit it and become bitter. If what we give others is kindness, then why would we deserve or accept less in return?

What we go through can be interesting, but how we get through it can be inspiring. Any of us can get entangled in a negative or destructive relationship or become a victim of unaddressed issues. The victorious victim is not ashamed of the shameful things that happen to them. I chose to see the confusion of those who shame victims and not accept it as my own. I seek to let go of misplaced blame.

We can practice spiritual martial arts by seeing the hurt beneath our anger and stepping out of the way of the aggression of others. This means we have to love some people from a safe distance. Let us not regret difficulties by keeping in mind the harder our struggles, the more inspirational we are when we rise above them. We can give our struggles a higher purpose using the strength we gain to help others, which transforms adversity into an advantage.

Before I left, our family therapist, who had known me for decades, said, "You've tried everything dignified, and you are extremely creative." I do not regret that I gave him multiple chances. I am not ashamed that it took time for me to accept that it might always feel like my love was falling into a black hole. Bottomless pits can be created by the betrayals of trust we all endure if we do not heal those wounds. No matter how patient we are, we cannot heal anyone else; we can only heal ourselves.

There can be places so dark within us that not even the light of another's love can illuminate them.

Years after I left, I sent an email offering a way to heal the damaged trust in the family by listing the things that I believe broke trust between us. I am not sharing it because I have no wish to engage or shame. I forgive it all, but trust can only be restored by admitting what happened, showing concern for feelings, and apologizing. I hoped he would acknowledge and apologize to me and our son, who has not spoken to him since before we left.

He described what I always told him felt like insulting public humiliations as teasing me, still minimizing the hurt and embarrassment his words caused me. I did appreciate that, for the first time, he wrote to me and acknowledged that he competed with me. I think he did not want me to have my own resources, believing if I did not have my own funds, I could not leave him. But I did not get with him for money, so I was not going to stay for lack of it. I was with him for love, but self-love must not be sacrificed.

Each of us has to overcome our own fears in order to give our love to others. If we do not heal ourselves, our fear will try to control them. Ironically, the unaddressed fear of losing someone can cause us to act in ways that may cause us to lose them. When those close to us do not show concern for our feelings, we can either shrink or get away from the crippling effects of not feeling safe or cared for. Some are not willing to do the work that healing requires. Others do not find the courage to be self-effacing. Admitting we are wrong paradoxically comes from trusting we are lovable anyway. I hope for him that it happens. I wish him peace, but no longer at my expense. I try not to give up on anyone, but I am willing to let go of fruitless struggles. My peace must not depend on anyone's response.

I knew I had to change my life, realizing taking care of his needs meant I had nothing left for myself, let alone others. By staying, I would have forsaken not only my own artistic fulfillment but the many who could possibly be helped if I shared my work with the world.

All nine attorneys I consulted with over our fourteen-year-long divorce told me I had no legal rights. Each time I replied, "I mean your profession no disrespect, but we all know there is a

249

right that is above the law—honor—and that is where I live. No one is above the law, but honor should be!" I think we all feel how important it is. Perhaps that is why we refer to the judge as your honor.

For my self-esteem, I needed to stand up for what was right no matter how painful it became. At the court-required bench bar conference, there were seven attorneys and me in the room. One said, "You guys have been at this for a long time."

"Yes, so long I have a joke," I said to the room full of expressionless faces. I continued, "How do you divorce an attorney?" I gestured to an attorney on either side of me, saying, "You hire two." I knew some of them would think I was crazy, but I needed to demonstrate the unfair system prejudiced against me could not break me. I had a family attorney on one side and a civil attorney on the other side because we were together sixteen years before we married.

Our twenty-one-year-old son insisted on coming to the next hearing knowing my attorney could not be there, as I had only been given a day's notice. Our son bravely went up to his father outside the courtroom before the hearing to say, "Dad, please don't do this."

We both recall his attorney arguing at that scheduled hearing something like, due to the shortness of their marriage, he should not have to give her much, or anything.

When the judge asked me, "Who is sitting next to you?"

Bodhi answered, "Their son!" My ex's attorney's assistant smiled behind her as Bodhi spoke. We were encouraged that the assistant appeared delighted that our authenticity became my innocent defense.

Having his child gave me no legal right to anything we created together. No economic value was assigned to all the artistic work I did to every inch of the interior of our house, which attracted a tour from the Museum of Modern Art in San Francisco. My artistic painting, stenciling, etched glass, copper stair rails, window treatments, decor and furniture designs were everywhere. No monetary value was given to the sixteen years of taking care of him, the family, the house, and whenever he asked for help with his business. While our adult son speaking up gave me no legal advantage, it may have undermined his attorney's tactic to keep the focus on our short marriage instead of our long relationship.

Some know how to manipulate and take advantage of those who do not have the funds or knowledge of the laws, but that does not make it right. It was a painful realization that the law is not about right, truth, or honor but about creating order. The first laws were the right of might.

During the exhausting years he had the house on the market, he allowed me no say in how, when, or by whom it could be shown, while I had to keep it spotless and available anytime someone wanted to see it with a few hours notice. We were not even allowed to be seen leaving. No one but us knew none of the appliances worked or that we did our laundry in the bathtub and kept the refrigerator cold with ice blocks. We could not use the oven, dishwasher, or microwave. We called it camping in the castle.

I did not feel safe after he spanked me in front of our ten-year-old son. I was not willing to have a lockbox on the front door allowing him to enter anytime he wanted. So I had to open the house and leave without being seen every time someone viewed the house. We were allowed one closet to lock all our personal belongings in.

I was spent emotionally, mentally, and physically by the ordeal. This was the first time I had been shaken to my core since being raped and getting pregnant at sixteen. Some betrayals of trust break us. Disappointment can put cracks in our heart that our hope can leak out of, and only love can restore us. My situation had been excruciatingly difficult, but losing the support of women friends made it almost unbearable. Many were accustomed to me being available for them. Some were even frightened or angry that it was not about them anymore. Others saw only what he showed everyone else—a wealthy gentleman letting me live in the big house. There were those unwilling to see my reality of always working and being frugal without ever getting paid or anything put in my name. Some were even jealous of what they imagined my life to be instead of seeing for sixteen years I was devoted to him and the family but did not even own my vehicle or have any money in the bank.

Women can believe they need to make compromises to survive in a world that discriminates against us. Some do not want to see their reflection in a woman who does not compromise and will find fault with her instead of the sexist world. I did not know until I needed emotional support that only the women I met at the abused women's meetings understood. They said I should write because it could help others. So here I am, hoping that sharing my story of healing and recovering my strength can help others regain theirs. It took distance for me to see that many were scared seeing me shaken, as I had always been strong. Instead of admitting they did not have the capacity to be there for me, some criticized me. During my most difficult times, I heard some of the most hurtful things of my life. I will not include these comments because my mother's voice inside says, "It is hard to be strong, dear, but you are, so you can forgive them," and I did.

When I was still with my son's father, I was offered a video contract. Because my ex had been an entertainment attorney, I asked him to look it over or recommend someone who would. I ended up finding my own attorney in the phone book. Thank goodness for my self-respect and perhaps good karma because that attorney years later said she was concerned for me divorcing an attorney. She asked a great family attorney to take my case. Then that family attorney recommended a civil attorney to write a palimony suit to pressure my ex to finally make me a settlement offer. But before it was all over, we had to get yet another attorney, a mediator who was both a real estate and family attorney, so I then had to pay three attorneys' fees. My attorney predicted correctly that my ex would finally make an offer in order to look good in front of that high-priced male mediator.

All the attorneys said we would get to stay in the house because he had so much debt against it, and considering the enormous deferred maintenance, it would cost him too much to force us out. We wanted to stay and resume our money-making endeavors of creativity retreats and video projects. We had not been able to do them for the years the house was on the market. But instead of letting us stay, he made me an offer, saying if I moved every item out by 2:30 p.m. nineteen days later, he would give me a settlement.

We moved things methodically from the bottom up seven levels to the driveway, clearing every item collected over two decades of raising a family there, including my framing and art equipment, tools, and supplies, plus the gigantic amount of stuff people had donated over the years for my creativity retreats. I was exhausted, and I injured my back. At 2 p.m., we pushed out onto the driveway what we could not get into the vehicle and drove away never to return.

He sent his worker to change the locks at precisely 2:30 p.m., but before he did, he found some prints I missed and put them in his truck. He asked me to meet him by San Quentin State Prison to give them to me. Perhaps if I had not been kind to him during his divorce years earlier, I would not have met the terms of our agreement and gotten my settlement after fourteen years of standing up for myself. I thought meeting in the prison parking lot was spiritually ironic because my ex always called our home The Big House—a nickname for prison. I called it the Seven Levels Sanctuary, but it did feel like a prison break by the end. We followed my attorney's advice. "Take it and disappear."

When it was all over, I think my lawyer felt bad at the way I'd been treated and that she could not make it easier or fairer for me, and she said, "You are everything the system does not respect."

"What am I?"

"A woman, an artist, without money, and spiritual."

"It is a good thing I respect myself."

Only wealthy white males wrote the constitution. The laws are still mostly written and enforced by this demographic and are understandably biased toward them.

My attorney told me she was shocked that I accepted his settlement offer so quickly after such a lengthy ordeal of a divorce. She had experienced divorcees being attached to the conflict, but it was his first and only settlement offer that I could recall. Perhaps there were others the attorneys did not share because they were unacceptable. It was not what I believed was mine all those years—half of the value of the house, without the mortgages, he got and used as he wished, or any of his development projects. But it was enough to start over and I wanted peace, which could not happen where I felt I was being treated so disrespectfully.

I believe if we think we can find the strength to get through difficulties, then we do. Our family therapist appointed

253

by the court to watch over my younger nephew when I was given guardianship of him decades earlier said, "You are an incurable optimist."

"Should I seek a cure?"

"No! You should bottle it and sell it." That could be a description of my artwork—me recovering my happiness by expressing the hurts, clearing the disappointments, and getting back to natural enthusiasm. This allows me to have no regrets, even about the toughest stuff I went through. Offering what I learned to others to help them through their struggles gives my pain a higher purpose.

I commit not to compromise what should not be compromised and treat everyone with respect. I love the respectful up close, the indifferent at arm's length, and the disrespectful from a distance, but I refuse to hate. I will not let cruelty make me cruel or let malice live in my heart. I do not give up on anyone or my own sensitivity. Instead, I am committed to sharing it with the world. Innocence and kindness can make us a target, but we must appreciate these admirable qualities, not forsake them. To turn difficulty into good, we must accept we did not deserve it. It is the victimizer who should take responsibility for their actions, not the victim. Society needs to stop blaming victims, and we all need to accept anyone can be one. The Buddhists say, "Do not feel sorry for the victim, because their karma has been purified by the assault. Feel compassion for the victimizer, as they have created bad karma for themselves."

Even my ex said my only addiction was turning everything into good. It is not an addiction; it is a choice. I choose to try to find some good in everything, especially difficulties. Overcoming my challenges I found great appreciation, without it, nothing is good, with it, anything can become meaningful. I gained some hard won wisdom to help others overcome their struggles. Some lose what is most important—to gain money or power. I won what is most important—self-respect and the respect of the honorable. Following luminous love out of the darkness of disappointment I found my courage to leave the sanctuary under siege and now I am bringing my dearest dreams into the light.

254

Eurasian Cranes Flock At Dawn

51
In Search Of True Beauty

I have lived in more than thirty five different places, including a tent, a teepee, out of my tiny Renault Dauphine car, and in an abandoned building. Someone who heard a story I told about a time when I had no home said, "You were homeless." I had never thought of myself that way because I have always been kind and helpful, so I had people offer me shelter when I needed it. But when my longest relationship dissolved, no one really understood my need because I had lived in a huge house with big views for nearly two decades.

I am grateful for every step of the journey that got me to safety and serenity. I believe appreciation is a great gift we can give ourselves.

I went from broken by the betrayals of trust to human Kintsugi, the Japanese art form of putting objects back together with golden joinery better than before. The process of putting ourselves back together is about turning broken into beautiful. My healed wounds became my story, and sharing them gives the pain a higher purpose. Bodhi told me that he went from feeling the loss of the only home he knew to feeling at home everywhere. As we set out to turn our adversity into advantage, we felt fortunate to have each other—someone who understood what we went through and the effort it takes to come out the other side. There were painful things that had to be discussed to come to understand them on the way to forgiveness and letting them go.

Twenty-two-year-old Bodhi and I took only what we needed: food, clothes, art tools, and a spirit of adventure and left everything unessential behind, especially the disappointment. Lightness began replacing heaviness as soon as we left the big house of hurt. Setting out into the unknown of our future unfolding was scary and exhilarating.

Knowing we needed time to heal, we decided to take four seasons as nomads before we chose where to settle. We named our rolling twenty-five-foot-long home "The Reasoned Manor," so we could relocate in a reasoned manner. Instead of lamenting we did not have a home, we turned it into an opportunity to explore the country and heal ourselves. Many people said we were living their dream. We set out to transform the nightmare siege of the sanctuary into a lovely dream, and so we did. Facing our fear of the unknown, strangers, and discomfort, was invigorating and empowering.

Reconnecting with friends and forty relatives was replenishing. Meeting people who cared about others and the environment, like the conservationists, was reassuring. Following the migrating cranes across the country was inspiring. Searching for true beauty was a journey to quiet our minds that had been in a defensive mode for way too long.

I chose to find a positive purpose in every negative feeling. Disappointment is hard, but it taught me that not everyone can be trusted, but I can come through hard times stronger with more understanding. Even in places I have never been before, I can be safe by staying aware of my surroundings. Simply quietly moving away from dubious people without calling attention to me or Bodhi kept us from having any traumatic events in a year at different locations. We had the essentials with us, so we did not have to stop anywhere we did not feel safe. We did not eat fast food once that year. We did eat at Chinese buffets but avoided the sushi when we were far from the ocean. Often driving all day, we would search the web for an RV park we could reach before dusk so we could survey our surroundings while it was still light. Bodhi always hooked up the utilities while I stayed inside preparing a meal. I have learned over the years that I can be a magnet for opportunists. We agreed it was best if no one knew who else was in the RV as a precaution.

Once when I was wondering why I have had so many dubious people drawn to me and thinking I might be doing something to attract them, seven-year-old Bodhi said, "Mom, you attract everyone because you are nice, so of course you attract bad guys too." Everyone prefers nice people, even predators. We all give off vibes. We cannot have animals, children, and innocent people trust us without also giving off the impression that we could be an easy mark. I do not want to go around projecting toughness, so I take precautions instead. To counteract my magnetism that attracts narcissists, I learned to give a little and see what comes back before giving more. To stay safe, I project confidence, like I know where I am going. I befriend safe people, so I have backup just in case. Opportunists, predators, and psychopaths look for easy prey like lions look for those at the edge of the herd. Being a friendly recluse, I have learned to move into the middle when I am in potentially dangerous situations. I talk to people so they can come to know me, care about me, and warn me if there is something I need to be aware of.

To increase the serenity and productivity in my life, I had to accept that I used to be kind to a fault, giving to everyone in need. I thought that was kindness, then I realized that the takers rush up front and take everything they can and do not share it with others. So I changed my prime directive to, "Give to the givers, and invite the takers to take leave so the givers can give it up!"

In my immaturity, I thought spiritual meant giving to everyone. Now I understand that if I give to those who give to others, kindness keeps expanding. The kickass kindness comes out if innocence is threatened, like a taser of truth. My older nephew described me as double tough.

I asked, "What is that?"

"Tough defends itself; double tough defends others."

Truth can be the most powerful weapon. Being honest with self first, then sharing what needs to be spoken can be a sword of truth cutting through falseness, revealing what needs to be seen.

I was drained by our sanctuary being under siege for so long, with no one but our son standing up for me, in a system that does not respect me, but I was not broken. I knew I needed to be reminded there are good, kind, humble people in this world, and I needed to find them and be with them.

My fear of not having a stationary home was replaced by the excitement of discovery. Giving ourselves the gift of being fully awake by getting plenty of regular rest along the way was key to staying safe. Discovering true beauty is a curious mind and an open heart, sharing the joy of doing our artwork along the way with a world in need of it.

Nature recharged us with deserts, plains, mountains, villages, lakes, and coasts. Our journey refilled our wells of inspiration. The adventure to find our place in the world meant asking ourselves, what is true beauty? We agreed it would be a place where people value one another and treat each other and the environment with respect, where people collaborate to do positive work. A place where we could do our creative work and share it with a community that appreciates it. Somewhere we can flourish and give our best to the world.

Many wonderful times on our journey were quiet moments, taking in the slowly changing landscapes. Along the miles of meandering roads without specific destinations or deadlines, our conversations were given the openness to flow naturally. We spoke about our dreams and curiosities. Pondering how to channel our passions into work that others will appreciate while being good for the world became our recurring theme. Committing to writing this collection of stories happened somewhere along the way from one side of the country to the other. Hearing I was living many people's dream made me wonder how we transformed our nightmare into our dream. It was a relief to move away from the city voted snobbiest in the nation.

I did not imagine Bodhi and I would be leaving together when he was young, but by the time I finally got my settlement so I could go, he was twenty-one, and I was delighted he wanted to go on this healing adventure with me. There is more of the type of abuse I endured in that county than any other, so leaving it behind was wonderful. The solitary confinement during the sanctuary under siege years in contrast to the wide-open space during our trip was profound.

The big spaces between thoughts let huge feelings surface and float away. Visiting the varied communities of this nation was enlightening. We experienced how connected we all are with much more in common than different. Easily finding kind people wherever we went was restorative after the elitist community of selfish show-offs we left behind. It was reassuring to find good folks wherever we went. I became thankful Bodhi's father broke all his promises, and we were forced to move because we could experience the generosity of strangers, which helped us forget the years of dealing with real estate brokers, lawyers, judges, and developers.

We met sweet people everywhere we went. All the different places had things in common. People are generally kindhearted, curious, and generous, from the cowboy town Medora, North Dakota, to bike rides in Yellowstone, hikes in Mammoth, the pirate festival in St. Augustine, Florida, dinner at the Wayside Inn in Sudbury, Massachusetts, driving through the Grand Tetons and all the little towns in between.

It was dawn on the rim of the Grand Canyon when the magnificence filled me with true beauty. The grandeur of the natural loveliness humbled me. My heart was overflowing with the mystery of our unlikely world in this vast universe. In the presence of such splendor, my human struggles dissolved. Witnessing how the great rock walls were cut by patient water reduced me to my essence. I felt an understanding that the constant water of kindness can cut through the hardest rock of remorse. I would no longer be diminished by anyone.

After four seasons rolling twenty thousand miles through forty states, my adult son and I chose a little big city on the north shore of Lake Superior to make our home. This is where I feel I should be, and we are both flourishing here. I have no regrets about the path to get here, only gratitude we are here. Fifty-two weeks of wandering the country, meeting marvelous people, taking in the varied terrain to choose where to settle. I said, "We both have to select where to make our new home. Duluth is my first choice, but you have to choose it, too, so you will not be mad at me during the long, cold winter."

After our second visit, he said, "You were not exaggerating. I thought you were romanticizing, but people are as kind here as you said they were."

My time as a wandering nomad settled in that moment as my joy returned, and I saw true beauty all around me.

Feathers on Mat

52
Nomad Comes Home

After twenty thousand miles, forty states, and a year on the road staying in a hundred different places, we agreed on a place to make home. Pouring rose, jasmine, and lilac scents into the tiny perfume bottles from my travels was the extraordinary in the ordinary. This unremarkable event is worth remarking because I finally have the space in my life to do something simply because it delights me.

The nomadic family I was born into flowed around the United States from the desert to the sea, to the middle of the country, then the northwest, and back to the southwest. I did what children do, followed my family. Nomads keep moving not necessarily because they wish to, but to survive. They are looking for a safe place like everyone else.

At seventeen, I set out on my own, first to the desert, then the southwest, then northwest, then northeast, searching for sanctuary. During my wanderings I returned to check on my family. But only my mother ever felt like home. After leaving the place where I raised my family and thought I would live for the rest of my life, my adult son Bodhi and I set out to search for where to call home. We rested in nature and restored ourselves, taking in the true beauty all around us. We took video, photographs, wrote, and drew. One day Bodhi said, "We are a good team!" I agreed that our different skills and perspectives made a powerful combination. I was delighted to combine our hearts, minds, and creative energies when he asked me to work with him. I said yes, and he named us MotherSon Productions.

On my lifelong journey I have not given up hope because I focused on my mother's spiritual teachings, my adult son's unwavering support, my godmother Marilee's faith in me, my spiritual mother Josephine's appreciation, my spiritual father Jonathan's advocacy, my mentor Walter's respect, and my designer mentor Mattalyn's kind acknowledgment. My elder angels still guide and give me strength.

We all have angelic people in our lives. Sometimes it is a brief encounter, but that can be enough if we focus on their wisdom and allow it to help us keep moving toward our dreams. My dream has always been creating a safe, serene sanctuary where I can do my best work and offer it to the world.

In my twenties, the community here in Duluth said, "You will never go anywhere where you will be more appreciated," and they were right. The community acknowledged my artistic skills and supported me in teaching creativity without any formal training. I got to teach every grade level. The newspaper headline read, "Free Spirit at Home in Duluth," and an article on Christmas Day started with "Modern Day Nomad Makes Her Home in Duluth."

Now this community is my hero again, welcoming me back and appreciating the creative energy Bodhi and I bring. Home is now a place where we are celebrated for being ourselves. We are settled where we have the best chance of rising to our luminous potential. It is our obligation to keep searching for that place where we can shine.

Duluth is where I discovered the best I have to offer the world, my art, my heart, and my ability as a creativity coach to guide others on the way home to themselves to express and share their creativity. Duluth has given me the space and the inspiration to share my stories that so many have told me helped them.

Since being here, I've had the peace of mind to write this collection of fifty-two of my life stories, which Bodhi has been inspired to turn into cinema and has received several grants to adapt into a screenplay.

As I watched the director of Catalyst Storieroad explain why they chose Duluth as their indie TV festival home, I had a vision of my son making my story into cinema bringing jobs to the region. This felt so right as a way to repay the community's recognition and kindness toward me. I felt it must happen.

Is it coincidence or spiritual synchronicity that Catalyst chose Duluth after my movie-making son and I chose it as our home? This community deserves to benefit, as it is a hero in my story once again, restoring my faith in humanity. What we have accomplished since moving here is evidence of what can happen when we get away from those who hold us back. No one on their deathbed says, "I wish I made more money, owned more property or stuff." Instead, people wish they had not surrendered their dreams. If we forsake our dreams, we can break our own hearts. That is why I say, love those who would sabotage our expansion from a distance. I strive to have no regrets from wondering what might have been. I choose to invest in becoming the person I wish to be. I do not judge the results of following my passion by funds, fame, or anyone else's standards, but by the fulfillment I get from doing it. If my artwork does not repay me monetarily for the time I have invested in it, I still have succeeded because all the time I spent doing it filled me with peace, and I learned while exploring my curiosities. The contemplative time doing art allows us to distill information into wisdom.

This requires we have a safe place to manifest our potential. This list of achievements since selecting the north shore of Lake Superior is proof of it being an environment we can thrive in. We chose a well-built, century old property that was affordable because of all it's deferred maintenance. Then we restored it ourselves and made a video called "Polishing the Emerald Lady," documenting the process. To celebrate, we hosted the Duluth Preservation Alliance's Christmas Party, and later we were on their summer historic homes tour with eight hundred curious visitors.

I taught creativity at the University of Minnesota Duluth – University for Seniors, where Bodhi was also asked to do a lecture on filmmaking. Bodhi made a short film about human trafficking *No Hero*, in which we played all four characters. We did a year-long feature documentary on a local family and shot four music videos. Bodhi has written several screenplays. One of his short films, *Tall Ships*, was selected for the Duluth Superior Film Festival, and he received the best director award at the Duluth 48 hour film project.

The *Congdon Magazine* featured us with a cover article. I've held several creativity retreats at The Emerald Lady, The Women's Club, and the Mental Health Court and Drug Rehabilitation Court. Bodhi and I did a program for Woodland Hills Juvenile Justice Services where I cut stencils of "Peace" in forty-eight different languages and then made them into floor-to-ceiling banners with the residents.

At the Karpeles Museum I did an exhibition of fifty-two crane paintings, "Sentinels of Serenity, Cranes of the World," and a second exhibition of twenty-six regional "Warblers & Wildflowers." My art was selected for the *Pheasants Forever* catalog as their pollinator print of the year. We videoed a collection of fifty-two of my wardrobe and jewelry designs called "One World Woman." We launched a web series called "The Creativity Show." More important than all of these accomplishments is the gratitude I feel that I did not give up hope before getting here. If I stayed in the mansion with the big views held back by someone else's fear, my growth would be hindered, and all those who might be helped by sharing my story and work would also lose. It would have been selfish to compromise out of fear of discomfort and change.

The world needs us not to lose hope, and it needs every sort of person and their unique insights to be whole: grocery clerks, mail carriers, doctors, artists, philosophers, teachers, and scientists. We are all a necessary part of humanity being healthy.

If only the aggressive people run things, the world will not return to balance. When we all add our strengths, skills, and insights, we can recreate harmony. The sensitives need to offer their perspective.

Doing art is an act of hope. It is how I get through difficulties, expressing them creatively. My artistic meditations on nature are a way to share the healing power of both art and nature. I believe it is the best I have to give. Through sharing my struggles, I might help others to not lose hope that they can get through theirs. If we do not lose hope, we can become the guardians of our precious world, not its destroyer. If we choose to find the good in everything, including the tough stuff because it teaches us resilience, strength, and compassion, we rise above it all.

We can choose to live a more economical and ecological life and be good for the world. Each of us can waste less and appreciate more. Together we can choose to take no one and nothing for granted. Let us love easily and accept that we are all connected. May we strive to keep learning and be better today than yesterday. Remember, we could be wrong about anything, and being right is less important than being kind. May we keep our minds open and our hearts clear of resentment. I want to live in respect for everyone and everything, create more and consume less, and share joy.

Consciousness can be a source of torment or a reservoir of strength. I want to do something with the consciousness I was given.

Embrace the gift of life and find what I have that helps others no matter how difficult the path. It is not what we believe that matters; it is how we act. Let me live an admirable life.

May I rise above my challenges, turning my adversity into advantage, post-traumatic stress into post-traumatic strength so I can share my best with the world.

I am grateful for all the lessons of my father's dark sadness as well as my mother's loving light and all the grays in between, guiding this nomad home.

Cosmic Conch Shell In Space

Epilogue

When people have suggested that I write about my life, I have felt flattered and validated. In contrast, I have also felt burdened or resentful about revisiting painful memories. Through this project, I have come to deeply understand and appreciate we must feel it to heal it and let it go. This book gives my pain a higher purpose, growing from it, turning it to strength and sharing it, hoping to help others transform their disappointments. Accepting my vulnerability has been a way to survive, and sharing it is a way to thrive.

I am grateful for all those who suggested this book, my willingness to take on this major project, and especially my son, Bodhi, for his unconditional support along the way.

This book is a manifestation of my choice to use what I have to create what I want. I have the space to do this project. I want a life full of creative purpose. The stories I selected for this collection changed my perceptions—epiphanies that expanded me and hopefully will be of value to others. I try to find some good in everything. Doing this project during social distancing has allowed me to create some good in this time and turn adversity into advantage.

People say I should share my stories because I have learned forgiveness and found peace. I do not regret what I have been through, because having much to forgive has been a path to forgiveness. Everyone needs peace to deal with challenges and enjoy life.

May we all find peace and share it with the world.

About the Author

Clare's many years of creativity coaching confirmed what she believed to be true—artistic expression comes naturally. Unfortunately, many do not have it nurtured and can lose connection to their creativity over time. Clare credits her classically trained fine artist mother who was a major contributing factor in Clare staying connected to her imagination and always encouraged her to follow her inspiration. Clare is committed to helping others reconnect with, or strengthen their connection to their creativity as her mother did for her.

Her mother referred to Clare as the "elegant primitive" because of her self-taught refined style. She told her daughter, "The rules do not matter for you. You would just have to forget them if you learned them because you follow your instincts and figure it out. This is most unusual for artists. Many overwork their pieces. You stop when it's done. Keep trusting yourself, dear."

Clare's art portrays the sublimely simple designs of nature and the expanse of the universe. Her art comes from her reverence for natural harmony and her curiosity about the ineffable cosmos. Her art is influenced by the time we are in when living in harmony with nature is crucial. Clare's art inspires us to rise to our luminous potential as guardians of the environment and its creatures.

Creating with whatever she had to work with was her way to express anytime and be in creative reverie whenever possible. Her first memories were dancing, sculpting, and making assemblages of found objects in nature. She began writing poetic prose before she read a book. She designed and hand-painted clothing then made jewelry and accessories. Sumi-e ink brush became her first graphic art practice, then playing a porcelain flute as a meditation, then doing pen and ink line drawings of nature. She designed or created most of the things in her home— furniture and furnishings, dishes, floral and tabletop arrangements, window and wall treatments, art, framing, and displays. Recently, she added the art form that can combine all others—video with her movie-making son.

Though best known for her crane paintings, she paints everything from insects to outer space, classic to modern, in her unique dream-like realism style. With over 500 paintings, drawings, and etchings in her house, "The Emerald Lady," a guest said, "It is a living museum with the heart of a home." Clare was too busy creating to count her creations until recently for a video project. When her unique creations reached over 2,000, she understood for the first time why people say she is prolific.

Clare's first public showing was her glass etchings in the Park Point Art Fair, Duluth, Minnesota, in the 1970s. Since then, her art has been exhibited in a wide variety of venues from small cafes to fine restaurants and wineries, galleries, corporate headquarters of a number of Fortune 500 companies, the Natural World Museum of Art, the Karpeles Museum, the cover of the *Red Rose* catalog, and on the San Francisco Museum of Modern Art tours.

Her art, writing, and designs were published by Pomegranate Artbooks in her *Book of Cranes* after observing all fifteen species of cranes in person.

Her art was featured as the *Pheasants Forever* catalog pollinator print of the year in 2019.

270

Clare's work was added to the International Crane Foundation Gift Shop Gallery in 2020 and the Cornerstone Gallery in Baraboo, Wisconsin, in 2021.

Clare was asked to create and direct a performance art piece for the Napa Valley Arts Council, which she involved ninety volunteer artists in and she dedicated to world peace.

She did skate dance performances in San Francisco at "Give Peace A Dance," Fort Mason, Theatre Artaud, and the North Beach Poetry Festival.

Clare's cabinet and table were selected and sold at the Architectural Designers Showcase in San Francisco.

She has done a number of public and private readings of her stories and poetry, including on Public Radio. Clare was interviewed on the *Women of Vision* television show.

In her twenties, Clare was asked to begin teaching her interdisciplinary curriculum "Dancing into the Arts." She has worked with every grade level in public schools, at universities, psychiatric hospitals, drug rehabilitation centers, crisis shelters, juvenile halls, and with the participants and staff of mental health and drug courts. She has worked with therapists, probation officers, lawyers, judges, nurses, and many other types of groups and individuals.

As a creativity coach, she loves guiding people home to themselves. Her work is based on her experience that the greater access we have to our imaginations, the confidence to express it, and the courage to share it, the more we have to work with to enhance our own lives, hope, heal, and contribute to others and our world.

Afterword

As I descend the stairs every morning during this time of social distancing, I see my mother pouring her heart into the keyboard. Watching this labor of love become a collection of stories to help others not lose hope inspires me. It is an honor to help these powerful and positive stories reach you by making them into an ebook and paperback.

My mother's willingness to tell her stories is courageous. Witnessing the healing effect her stories have on others has long inspired me to share them by developing them into an episodic series.

Her story is about a self-taught person from a severely dysfunctional family who holds onto childlike wonder and overcomes enormous difficulties. Her's is a journey of a person who is not jaded despite having ample cause to be. The deprivation, instead of breaking her, empowered her to become a visionary artist. Difficulties fueled her artistry and motivated her to help others meet their challenges. The stories of my mother's childhood are about a lack of safety and certainty. Out of necessity, she became an adult child—a hub around which the damaged family wheel wobbled. The cacophonous chaos of her upbringing resulted in her choosing to try to make order from disorder. Her diverse and immense body of work came from her desire to create calm in the chaos. Her story shows someone confronting the darkest parts of humanity by staying in the light. Her mother wrote her a note inspiring the book's title, "Did you know you have inner incandescence, dear?"

The cover image portrays naked vulnerability and the weight of disappointments replaced by wings to rise above the darkness.

My mother's life stories demonstrate the powerful role attitude plays in processing trauma, transforming adversity into advantage. Moments of great impact have their effect, but whether we rise above or sink into them is influenced by our attitude. As she has said, do not regret difficulties; just turn them into art. Creative genius can be born from extreme adversity.

Watching my mother's dedication to her art, I learned from her profoundly simple practices. One of which she calls with wry humor, "The 7 Fs." Find something Fun, Follow it, Focus until you Finish, and Feel Fulfilled.

When she is overwhelmed, she organizes something, turning a little adversity into a big advantage. This practice allows her to be ready to act on inspiration when it comes. Her choice to express any feeling creatively results in healing because expressed feelings stimulate the immune system. Her commitment to this practice has made her a profound and prolific artist. This book is an example. It has helped me not lose hope. I trust it will help you keep hoping you can create a better life, and together we can create a better world.

Other Products By The Author

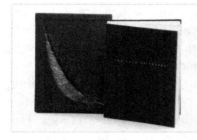

The Book of Cranes

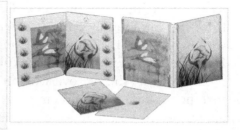

Crane Stationary

Crane Poster

To purchase any of these other products from the author please email ClareCooleyCollection@Gmail.com with "Book of Cranes" in the subject line.

15% Off Clare Cooley's Art Prints

We can provide you a 15% off promo code for a purchase on Clare's webstore www.ClareCooley.com/shop

If you would like this promo code please email us at ClareCooleyCollection@gmail.com and put "15% off promo code" in the subject line.

Creativity Coaching

Clare's recent Creativity Coaching clients include: University of Minnesota Duluth, University For Seniors, St. Louis County Drug & Mental Health Courts, the Duluth Women's Club, Lisa Fitzpatrick (Director of UMD VIZ & MMAD Labs) and Cathy Cato, BSN, MPH, Poet.

We can provide you a 15% off your first Creativity Coaching Session.

If you would like to take advantage of this offer please email us at ClareCooleyCollection@gmail.com and put "Creativity Coaching Promo" in the subject line.

Connect With Clare

For more information about this book and to join the mailing list go to
www.IncandescenceBook.com

To see "Life of Art" a short documentary about Clare's work, to take a virtual tour of Clare's Home Studio, "The Emerald Lady" and to see other videos from the video production company she started with her son Bodhi Werner go to
www.MotherSonProductions.com

See Clare Cooley's Webseries "The Creativity Show" go to
www.TheCreativityShow.com

Connect with Clare on Social Media
Facebook
      Facebook.com/ClareCooleyCollection
Instagram
      Instagram.com/Clare_Cooley_Collection
Twitter
      Twitter.com/ClareCooley

Acknowledgements

Facing my fear of shining by sharing my stories and some of the validating things people have said to me takes all the courage I can muster.

The socially acceptable self denigration many, especially women participate in, not only keeps us from rising to our luminous potential, but also does not help the world. The world is richer when we share our perspective. It should be celebrated to speak about what we alone can be an expert on, ourselves, and our stories.

May we face the fear of our own brightness and add our light to the world.

I would like to acknowledge all those who offered kindness, encouraging words, smiles, and hugs that kept me going, but there are too many to list.

Thanks to all of you who believed in me, helping me find the strength to get here. This book is due to your kindness. Deepest gratitude to each and every one of you.

Special Thanks

Barbara Layne
Shannon Booth
Sumner Matteson
Cathy Cato
Marko Eveslage
Ashley Turner
George W. Archibald
The International Crane Foundation
Clare Boisineau
Jill Bugbee
Josephine Landor
Jonathan Rice
Mattalyn Pitts
Walter Landor
Marilee Pazosa
Claire Kirch
Rosalie Uggla
Alev Croutier
Noelle Oxenhandler
Rose Boyajian
Claire Mirande
Photos by Bodhi Werner, Harold Hingle Photography,
Seraphina Landgrebe www.seraphina.com
Extra Special Thanks to Bodhi Werner
for Book Design & Production

Publishing this book was funded in part
by a grant from the Arrowhead Regional Arts Council.

Clare's Parents Leon & Barbara

Clare Doing Art

Teaching *"Dancing Into The Arts"*

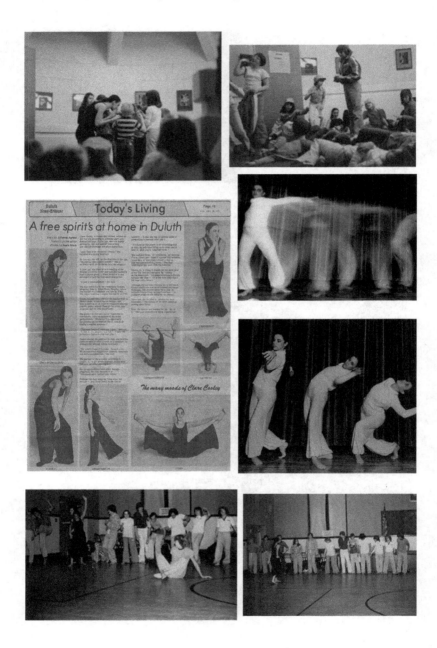

Clare Modeling

Gowns/Jewelry by
Mattalyn Pitts

Dance Performance

Music & Performance

Creativity Coaching

Clare & Her Art

Clare & Bodhi

THANK YOU

I'd appreciate it if you would share this book and review it.

www.IncandescenceBook.com

CPSIA information can be obtained
at www.ICGtesting.com
Printed in the USA
LVHW082026150721
692785LV00001B/3